SHATTERED
SOUL

K. Wieker

AN ANGEL PARENT'S JOURNEY

SHATTERED SOUL

KRISTINA WIDENER

TATE PUBLISHING
AND ENTERPRISES, LLC

Published by Tate Publishing & Enterprises, LLC
127 E. Trade Center Terrace | Mustang, Oklahoma 73064 USA
1.888.361.9473 | www.tatepublishing.com

Tate Publishing is committed to excellence in the publishing industry. The company reflects the philosophy established by the founders, based on Psalm 68:11,

"The Lord gave the word and great was the company of those who published it."

Published in the United States of America

ISBN: 978-1-68352-869-2
1. Family & Relationships / Death, Grief, Bereavement
2. Family & Relationships / Parenting / Motherhood
16.08.01

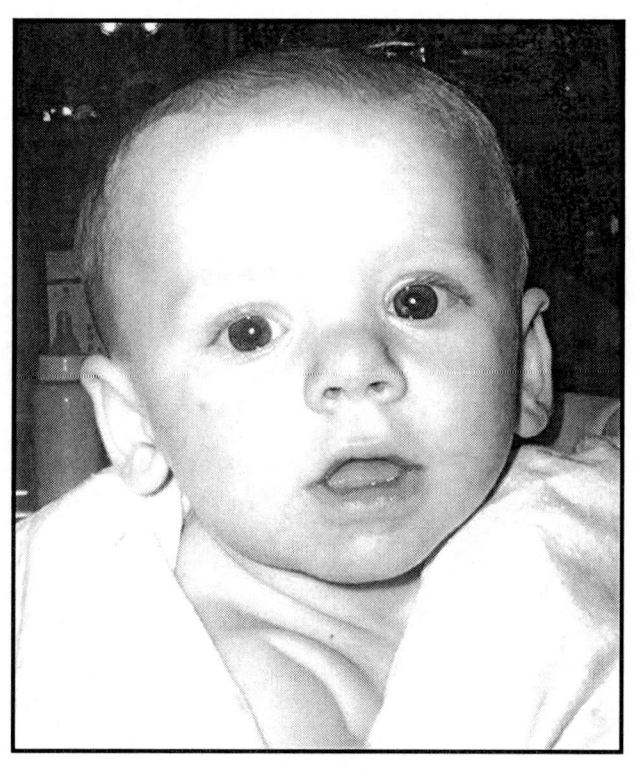

In loving memory of my son, Zackary Allen "Mr. Man" Gehring. My precious son, you were taken from me far too young at the age of five months. Mommy will always love you and miss you, Mr. Man. I will see you again on the other side. Until then, wait for me. I have things to do, and when my time is finally done, meet me with open arms.

To all the angels that left their loved ones far too soon, I hope that the memories of you fill the hearts of your families until they can once again hold you in their loving arms.

CONTENTS

INTRODUCTION

What you are about to read will very likely cause your heart to hurt and your soul to weep. It may very well make you want to hug your children or the children you hold close to your heart a little closer at night. What you are about to read is a true story. It is based on the events I have lived and still live every day. This is also a story that all too many others know, yet live in silence.

With this book...the silence can end.

Welcome to my journey.

This has been a road of pain, grief, discovery, loss, healing, joy, love, and so many other things that are hard to put a name on. This is my story, my version of the thoughts and feelings that I have experienced since losing my youngest child. That is a hard statement to say, to write, to read, but it is the cold fact of the matter. I will take you through the roller-coaster ride I have lived and am *still* living. I will tell you what I can remember, what I felt, and how I feel now at the time of writing this.

The time that has passed since the loss of Mr. Man measures in years now, and this process of mourning will be ongoing until the day I take my last breath. My life and those in it has changed from the beginning to the time of writing this, and I am sure that it will change many times before my days are done. I will try to be as honest as possible about the relationships, but this is not about those things entirely. This is about my journey, my grief, my coping—not about some of the smaller things and not about putting others down. Relationships end, and new ones begin. This is a fact of life. So the honesty will be there, but not the negativity.

Through this journey I have realized that nothing in this life is certain; regardless of how much we *want* to have certainties, we just do not get them. There are many things that you think you can count on, and when push comes to shove, those things are no longer there. On the other hand, there are many things that you realize have been holding you up, and you didn't even notice it. There are also those pleasant surprises that appear out of nowhere that show you a new side to life, that show you that life can be worth it again. Life worth living won't be easy. We need challenges to make us grow and become a better "us." We need the good to get through the bad, and the bad to appreciate the good.

Some things that I have written on these pages will seem very simple. What I mean by that is this: you will read the details as I know them, the facts as they had been given to me, and that is about it. The biggest part of that is because some of the memories are a little hazy in my mind, and so I can only relate to you what I know is certain in these instances. Everyone going through a trauma, as major as the loss of a loved one especially, has things that tend to get skewed a bit, specifically your memory. Sometimes it is time itself that gets skewed.

Through my life I have experienced moments that have seemed to stretch on far longer than they actually did in reality. There are other memories that I have that seem to be blips of time, yet in reality they were days or weeks. These have become more so the norm for me since losing my youngest son. There are events that have happened that I was so certain were over quickly, then when talking to others who were there, I realized that no, in fact, we were there many hours longer than I seem to remember. I also frequently hear the statement "It didn't take that long" when I am describing events that I may have thought or felt took hours, days, or even went on for weeks. So as we progress through this, I will try to explain how I felt, but also what I know of the facts so that you will hopefully be able to see how the events happened, but also how I viewed them.

Sometimes I have flashbacks, and they can be extremely fuzzy or have such clarity that I would swear I am reliving them again and again. Some things I remember for certain, others I merely "think" that is how it went. There are other moments that I can only recount to you what I was told. I will try to stick to the facts as much as possible, and I will tell you when it is something I am unsure of, or I will mention that the information comes from another source.

I will share some information about my family then, how it is now, and everything in between. It is true that the loss of a loved one changes that, but the loss of a child changes that tremendously more. The interactions I now have with friends, family, strangers, everyone really, is definitely different. I do not hesitate to say that I have three children, but when people only see two, I do have to explain. I then deal with the looks, the "I'm so sorry" statements, and the pity. The pity is the worst one to deal with and handle.

Now that you know a little about the "game plan," so to speak, let's just jump into the fray. I've always been the kind of girl to live by the philosophy of go big or go home. With that concept, this is *my* story of *my* pain, grief, sorrow, anger, and probably a million other emotions I don't know how to describe. These are all things that my heart, my body, and my soul learned and felt after the death of my youngest son, Zackary. This is *my* path of anger, of hurt. Of feeling lost, alone, and at the same time, still being thankful for what I have. This is *my* story of how I crawled out of the hole of despair I fell into and how I have decided to help others find their way through their own fog. This is how I have come to terms with a lot of the emotions that have coursed through my very being, and also how I have had to come to terms with the changes in my life since losing my youngest son. This is also my journey down a not-often-traveled road of grief as I pull my soul back together to find comfort, solace, and hopefully…meaning.

Follow me through this voyage that is still in progress. Come with me, inside my soul, as I search for meaning, comfort, and purpose during the darkest hours of my life. I heard this once: When you lose your parents, you are considered an orphan. When you lose your spouse, you are considered a widow. What do they call you when you have lost a child?

This is my journey to define that, to make sense of things, and to get back on the path I need to be on after losing Mr. Man. I call us Angel Parents. Every belief has some version or description of angels, and I honestly believe that our children are in a perfect place together, waiting for the day when they will be reunited with each of us.

Every word I have put into this book is a bit of healing, and the things I have done throughout this process, in many ways, a sense of closure. I will never have complete closure or full healing, but I can get as close as I can to both. Thank you for walking with me as I share Zackary's life, my joys, and my sorrows in the only way I know how.

Thank you for taking the time to read this, for being willing to walk this path with me, even if it is just for a short while. This story is how my son's memory will live on. Some of you are reading this because you know what this journey really is all about.

There are some that I am sure think I am doing it for attention, but what they do not understand is that I do this because I am still the mother of three children. Just because the average person does not see him, that does not mean he is any less my child. I say I have three children because I am not afraid to tell someone of my pain of losing Zack. I do not do it to gain pity or sympathy. I do it because my hope is that one day, the families that have had to live in silence for so long will feel that they can talk about their pain and grief.

I do this because I hope that one day, society won't look at this as being a taboo or off-limits topic and be able to be supportive of the families instead of secluding them. I do this in the hopes that future Angel Parents—and we know there will be future Angel Parents—will no longer have to live in silence about their pain. I do it in the hopes that my youngest son's memory will spread from one heart to another, and that through this pain and grief I'm experiencing, that perhaps others will find solace.

You will also notice that I frequently mention being with Zack again. Do not take this in any negative fashion.

I have too much to live for; I am not considering shortening my life. I certainly am not ready to leave my other two children yet. I have so many dreams I still want to live and experience, and I have too many others in my life that I am not ready to leave yet. However, the thought of being with him again is one of the biggest thoughts I have when it comes to Mr. Man. I won't be without him forever. I hope that you will be able to understand me and my viewpoint on this more after reading everything I have put on the following pages.

I was not "new" to this type of pain. I had been on the outside looking in with several friends and family members when they had a loss. I knew so many others that had lost a child to miscarriage, infant loss, accident, or illness. It was odd to me to realize that there were so many out there that had never had to deal with this type of grief. I easily know over a dozen parents that have been walking this path for longer than I have been. That was a frightening number to think about and realize that I was now a part of. Even more frightening was to realize that so many others I knew could not think of anyone *they* knew that had been through this tragedy. Another sad and amazing realization to me was that my youngest son's funeral was the first funeral in general that some people had ever been to. I have been to so many funerals in my life that I honestly can't count them all anymore. Funerals for family members of all ages, friends, acquaintances, and to realize that some people had never been to a single one absolutely floored me.

I also had to deal with the realization that some of my friends who have suffered miscarriages did not think that their loss was as great as mine. I still fight with this every day to make them realize that to me, the loss of a child is great and traumatic, regardless of the age. Among my friends that have suffered this loss, those that have had a miscarriage try to tell me that their loss is not as *major* as mine because they never got to hold their child. I disagree with that thought process. Those parents held their child, just not in their arms. A child will forever hold a place in your heart, regardless of their age, how long they lived, or how many times you held them. Comparing the loss of one child to the loss of another is like comparing apples to zebras. The comparison will never work and will never make sense because each child, parent, family, and group dynamic is completely different.

I have met others who have lost a child later in life when the child was in their teens or twenties, and they also have told me that to them, my loss is greater. I can't wrap my head around any of this. As a parent, I think that regardless of the age of your child, the loss is great and, in many cases, just as crippling to the core. Those that lose their child when he or she was older, I hear, "I was able to have all those years with my child. You didn't." I do not think that matters either. They had more time to build memories, and the loss of more memories still hurts just as deep.

I believe that the loss of a child, at any age, is a pain so deep that it is felt in your very soul, and regardless of the age of the child, they will always be your baby. I see it so often among grieving parents that they try to downplay their grief by saying that someone else's grief is worse. I am guilty of this as well. I think we need to stop focusing on that and focus on the fact that we are all connected in a messed up sort of way because we have lost one or more of our children. We need to come together and support each other, which should include ourselves, because in a sense, we are not giving enough meaning to the memory of our children. Each of our children was as important as any other, and we need to come together to honor their memories and hold each other up.

This book is in memory of my youngest son, but it is also for those out there that need to know that they are not alone. I hope that after you read this, you find *something* in it. Even if that something is so small no one else would notice, as long as you found something, then I know that reliving these memories was all worth it.

Every Angel Parent has a different story to tell. Some are miscarriages, some are accidents, others are more heinous, and then there are those like myself, which involve SIDS/SUIDS. Each one is different, but the similarities to each other of the emotions that have been felt cannot be denied. This is my journey down the path of the tragic loss of my youngest child, how I have coped with it through every step and every up and down. I am a survivor, and this is one more step in that survival. There are many more to come, some steps I'm not even aware of yet, others that I know are right around the corner. Regardless of what the future holds, what steps may come, what setbacks I may have, I will make it. My family will make it. We will tackle the steps as they come, and in the end, when my last days are upon me, I will be able to face that moment with the certainty that I survived.

Rachel, Zackary, and Devin—
the day Mr. Man came home from the hospital.

1

THE BEGINNING

My life has always been crazy. I have never been what you could possibly consider as normal. I tried normal once and did not like it; it was a horrible five minutes. *Simple* is a word that describes me, but not normal. I have been through trials and tribulations, and through each of them I came out standing strong and tall. I might not have been the same as I was before, but I was still me. However, nothing would prepare me for what I was to eventually experience.

Each thing I have lived through in my life has shaped and molded me in some way. Living with my grandparents always so close to us, even living with us at once point, helped me have a sense of how important family is. Each death of a family member taught me to appreciate the ones I love and to never take tomorrow for granted. Every ending sparked a new beginning in some way. Sometimes that new beginning is physical, other times it is only emotional or mental, and sometimes it is all three.

I had an average childhood with my siblings and my mom. We lived out in the country, or what I like to refer to as the "middle of nowhere." We had neighbors, family close by, and a decent backyard to play in. The town that we grew up in was fairly small, everyone knew everyone, and you felt safe. Nothing extraordinary ever happened. We used to joke that if you stood on one end of the town and said something, give it five minutes, and the whole town would know what you said.

My grandmother lived with us until she went to the nursing home when I was ten years old; she then passed away later that year in the nursing home. I remember growing up that we were never religious, but we were spiritual. My grandmother's teachings of simplicity in life, belief, and faith are what I have realized my entire mind-set is now built upon. Those simple teachings will stick with me, and I hope to be able to enrich the lives of my children with those same ideals.

I went to live with my father when I was fourteen simply because I was a rebellious teenager toward my mom. I thought I had all the answers. I moved back with my mom just under three years later and realized that I was an idiot with some things, and that my mom was so much more than just my mom. She was my best friend, my confidant, and my own little subconscious voice when I needed it. She was there to support me through graduating high school and encouraged me to look forward to the future with hopes and dreams for college, career, family, and chasing the sunsets.

I married my first husband when I was only eighteen, and while I do not regret that choice, it really was not the smartest move for me. Our relationship was failing, and we both should have seen that. However, when you are young and you *think* you love this person, you can't see the forest for the trees. My oldest son, Devin, was born just a few weeks after my nineteenth birthday. Devin had some problems shortly after he was born; at ten days old he had what the doctors called a "near SIDS event." I had laid him down for a nap and decided to take one myself. When I woke up, he wasn't breathing and was purple. I placed my hand on his chest, and he jerked, gasped for air, woke up, and his color came back.

I immediately called his doctor and told him to meet me at Toledo Children's Hospital, and then called my mom to have her drive us there. The next six months were filled with chaos because he was on an apnea monitor until shortly after he turned six months old. There were times I thought that monitor would go off simply because you looked at it wrong. The monitor was set for a specific range of heartbeats and respirations per minute, and if the child's level of either went too high or too low, the monitor would sound off. I learned a lot about patience through that whole ordeal, and I also learned to be thankful for the blessings I've been given.

My divorce from Devin's biological father was final in 2002, but to be honest, the marriage was over almost as soon as it began. We definitely were not suited to be together, and we spent more time apart than we ever did together. He and I have had issues over the years, but for the most part, we have tried to stay civil with each other. My relationship and divorce from my first husband taught me that I was capable of handling things on my own. I learned how to take care of schedules, repairs, budgets, and so much more. I was independent before I married him, but I was even more so during, and then after, the divorce. This was a stepping stone in my life and my learning. I didn't realize then what it was leading me to, and even if I would have known, I don't think there is anything I could have changed.

My mother was then diagnosed with cancer in April 2002, and her health went downhill fairly fast. The independence I learned was one of the things that helped me get through my mom's care. I took care of my mom up until the point that she went into the nursing home in April 2003. We had doctors' appointments, grocery shopping, runs to the store, and everything in between that needed to be done. I learned how to take care of the situation at hand, handle it, and then process it if need be. I also learned how to juggle all my daily activities that needed to be done while still being a functional single mom to Devin.

During the time of my mother being ill, my second husband and I started dating. Our courtship was a whirlwind amid all the activity of taking care of my mother, and we were married in May 2003. While it was quick, I was glad to be able to have my mother be a part of that day since just a short eighteen days after we said our vows, she passed away. You never really know what you're made of until you are forced to step up to the plate, and when my mom passed away, I really felt that I had now climbed the mountain of hardship and that I could start building my future and my dreams.

My second child, Rachel, was born in 2008, and then my third was Zackary in 2009. My children are the apples of my eye, each in their own way. I refer to Zack as Mr. Man. I'm not sure why that was the choice or why it stuck, but it just suited him. Rachel has been called Bug or Cuddle Bug almost since the beginning, but definitely before she was born. Finally, Devin's nickname, thanks to Rachel, is Dodo. She couldn't say his name for the longest time, so one of the aunts "helped" her come up with Dodo. It has now stuck with him, and every little kid calls him that, and it makes Devin beam with pride.

At this point, I have what I think is going to be it. I have been through hardships, tough times, and loss, but I was as happy as I thought I could be, and I had three amazingly beautiful children. I finally graduated from college like I promised my mom, and things were starting to go somewhere. I felt that nothing was left to go wrong. Things weren't perfect, but I felt that with hard work, we could make it work.

While I thought that nothing else could go wrong, I was soon to realize how flawed that thought process was.

They say not to count your chickens before they hatch, and that was a harsh lesson I wish I never had to learn. This is the story of that lesson and many lessons to come since. I remember a saying my mother told me when I was very young, no idea who the author is: "We the willing, led by the unknowing, are doing the impossible for the ungrateful. We have done so much, for so long, with so little, that we are now qualified to do everything with nothing."

That statement now makes sense…

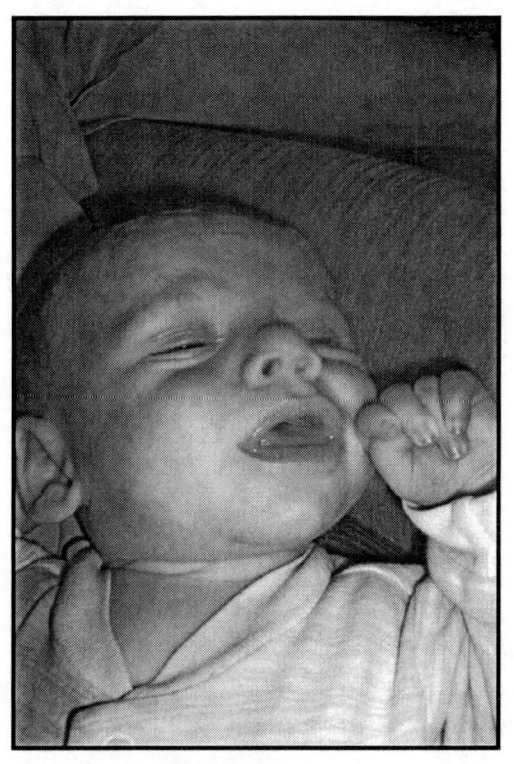

A slightly fussy Mr. Man.

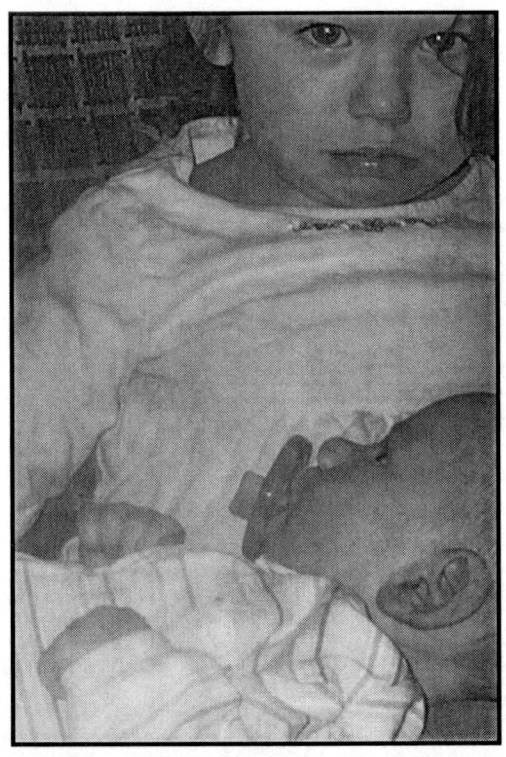

Rachel and Zackary—do you think she was
slightly protective of her little brother?

2

THEN

To completely understand the events that have unfolded, you need to understand me and my family, or at least how I defined it at that time. My biological family consists of myself as the youngest, with one brother, David, and one sister, Kara. My extended family is extremely large. My mother was the youngest of eight children, and her siblings took "Go forth and multiply" as a serious credo in their lives. I grew up with cousins always being a big part of life, aunts and uncles everywhere, family gatherings, and grandparents loving on us. My parents divorced when I was young, and I didn't know my father's side of the family very well, so I really only have memories of my mother's side.

Family means many things to different people, and for me, family is not just a biological bond, but a bond with a mix of those that not only I have chosen to be in my life, but that have chosen me as well. Usually the family that you *choose* is closer to you because a relationship has to be formed, not just given by blood.

Now that family I had at the time was bigger than most can imagine. There were more than half a dozen "sisters," and then add to that their husbands and children. There were even more that were not geographically close, but still members of our "family" regardless. At the time, that consisted of more than twenty children ranging from over twenty years old down to infancy. This does not begin to cover the full scope, but this gives you an idea of the large group of people that I considered family.

Some of the most prominent people in our lives would be my sister Kara and her family. My sister and I have had our ups and downs over the years, but for the most part, we still try to stay close. Heather and Mike, along with their children, are just amazing individuals. I couldn't ask for better people to love me and my family, and I can't ever explain to them just how much I love them. This is just an example of a few members of this large family, and there is no way that I can name them all in one sitting.

This large group at that time was the reason I had days of being crazy as a loon, yet the next moment they helped me keep it together. We didn't always see eye to eye, but we would work through our differences and come out at the end of the tunnel better than when we started. This amazing group was my support system and something that words can't describe, but you know what it means in your heart.

So there I was, in the middle of this mixture of people I called family, married, three kids, and lots of plans. We were oblivious to the future, as everyone is, and we were living in the now. I was amazed at watching my children, their unique personalities, their interactions, and seeing the world differently through each of their eyes. If I had only known then a fraction of what I know now, I could have prepared myself for something…for anything.

The unfortunate thing is that not only did we not realize the hell we were about to go through as an immediate family, but also the changes that would happen in our larger family. Changes are always going to happen, and it is how we handle those changes that shows our relationships, makeup, and where we've been. This isn't to say anything negative; it is pointing out that not everyone is built to handle certain changes. It is one of the things that makes each of us unique and as individual as a fingerprint. Remember, that change not only affects you, it affects everyone you know, some in a positive way and others in a negative way. Change is, in essence, the only true constant in life. Remember that with each change in life and how you proceed from each one.

Mr. Man for president!

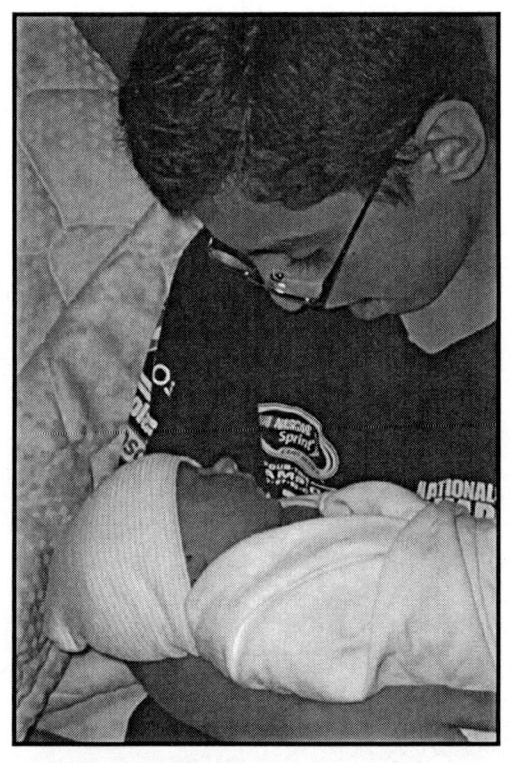

Devin with Mr. Man. He was so happy to have a
little brother, his wish list was complete!

3

MY MR. MAN

Zackary was just an adorable little boy. I know, since I am his mom I should think that, but when everyone told me so, I don't think it was just me. He was so interactive from just a few days old that you began to see the little personality forming from day one.

Zack was born in the evening of Saturday, December 5, 2009, after thirteen hours of labor. He weighed in at seven pounds and fourteen ounces and was just over eighteen inches long. His hair was so fine, straight, and blond that he looked bald, and he was absolutely gorgeous. Of my three children, he weighed the most but was the shortest in length. I thought it made him look adorably pudgy.

When Zack was examined by the pediatrician shortly after birth, she decided to put him on oxygen for a short time because the readings of his levels were a bit low. She said that room air was just slightly less oxygenated than what he was needing. We were told that this was pretty typical, so we didn't worry too much about it. Before long, he was off the oxygen, and everything was right in the world again. All of the tests that they do on newborns came back great; no issues anywhere to be seen. The morning after Zack was born, I went through the surgery to have my tubes tied, and the next day, Monday, we were both discharged in good health to go home.

Everything we did with Mr. Man was a new adventure. When we would put him in his swing, he would sit and giggle for what seemed like forever. He would start to doze off, giggle, nod off, giggle, and repeat. He was so comical to watch, all of his movements, facial expressions, sounds, everything about him was just a joy to me, as it was with my other children, but they were each unique, and I loved every bit of it.

Devin loved being a big brother and would sit and snuggle with both Rachel and Zack. You would think that Devin was the king of the world with his siblings snuggled up to him. He didn't like everything about having babies in the house, like the crying and dirty diapers, but he loved his brother and sister more than you can imagine.

It is really hard for me to describe the idiosyncrasies of an infant because everything I say sounds totally biased, but he really was an incredible little human. The interactions he had with anyone and everyone was just amazing. He would respond to anything you said to him, and you would swear he completely understood what you were saying. He had this full range of facial expressions that was hilarious to watch. Zack even recognized who was interacting with him by looking toward them, different facial expressions for certain people, or noises he would make. His expressions were even more obvious when you saw his eyes; they were the most absolute gorgeous shade of blue that reminded you of an icy-colored sky. If the eyes are really windows to the soul, then Mr. Man had an amazing soul that he shared with all of us.

We enjoyed Zack's first Christmas together as a family, even though he was only three weeks old. It was a time of family gatherings, talking, eating, and everyone playing with the kids. Everyone enjoyed passing Zack around since he was the youngest and definitely quite the snuggle buddy. It seemed that after Zack was born, we all looked for reasons to get together. We had a bit of a snag in things when I was hospitalized shortly after the New Year with gallbladder issues. That was a tough time of having to be away from my children, especially a newborn. Friends and family really stepped up and helped out so that I knew that there was nothing to worry about during my hospital stay and then ensuing recovery from surgery.

We eventually got into a pattern that was as simple as we could get it: Devin off to school, Rachel and Zack at home during the day, housework, family time after Devin got home from school, dinner, bedtime, repeat. It really is amazing how much we take for granted when things follow a normal pattern or routine.

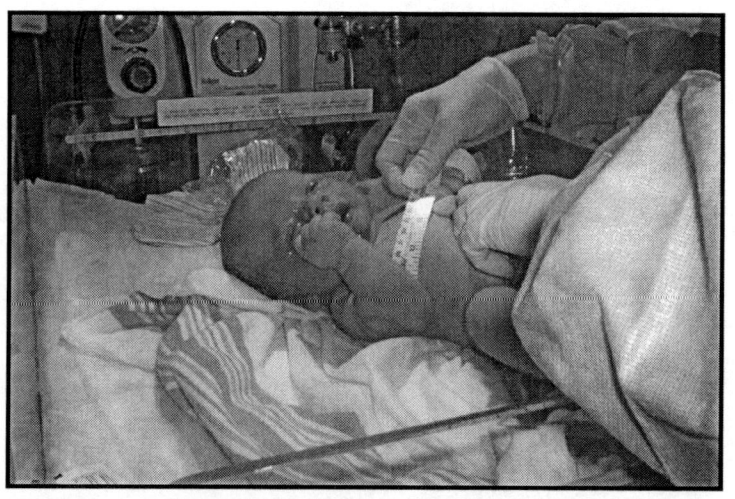

Mr. Man not being very cooperative with
the nurse right after he was born.

4

Reality Happens

The morning of Tuesday, May 11, 2010, was just like every other morning. Rachel went to sleep late, Zack woke up early, and Mommy didn't get much sleep. I did my best to keep the little ones from waking Devin up since he needed his sleep and he also had school. Zack woke up like every other morning, around 5:00 a.m. for a diaper change, play for a little while, and then take a bottle. Same as it had been for months with no change.

We played, I sang, changed his diaper, fed him his bottle, and we played some more. I made up a song for him one night when he first started teething that always calmed him down and made him giggle. This little song made him happy, and a happy baby makes a happy mommy. Using the tune of "I'm a Little Teapot," I would sing this song:

I'm a little grump butt, short and chubby
Here is my butt, and here is my tummy
When I get all ticked off, I will shout
So bend me over and squeeze the gas out.

Over the course of his teething, the song changed slightly. I needed to add another verse to keep his attention going along with it so he didn't get bored:

I'm a little grump butt, yes, its true
You love me, and I love you
I am getting teeth in, not one but two
So I'm gonna scream until they come through!

Of course we had dancing we would do with the song, and it never mattered why he was slightly upset; every time I would sing that song, he would quiet down right away and listen to me sing. That Tuesday morning I probably sang that song what felt like a hundred times, just to hear him giggle and see him smile. He finally fell asleep around 6:30 a.m., and I decided to get some shut-eye.

Devin was home from school that day, and he helped handle the little ones for most of the morning so that I could get some rest since I had been up most of the night. This was a fairly normal day, nothing unusual, the "same stuff, different day" syndrome.

That afternoon we had to go to the store to pick up a few things, and Devin watched both little ones like he had done several times. When we got home, Rachel was playing, and Zack was taking a nap.

Rachel was being a typical toddler that afternoon, running around having a "terrible twos" moment. Zack was taking a nap on Devin's bed since it was closer to all of us, but that also meant that Rachel was closer to him as well. She was notorious for trying to wake him up to play with him; she never understood that Zack was still too little to play with his big sister. She always tried to say that he was "her baby," and when I would disagree, she was not a happy camper. Devin was in the kitchen making a sandwich for both him and Rachel. Almost as if on cue, she went in to try to annoy her baby brother. He woke up a little bit, but Devin got to her before Mr. Man fully woke up, and he was able to usher her out of the room. I said words to Devin that I will never forget, and still in some ways it haunts me: "If he fusses too much, bring him here."

Zack made a few noises, snuggled down on the bed, and went back to sleep. Devin was pretty proud that he was able to head a fussy session off at the pass.

That was the last noise he made, the last thing he did. Devin had gone back to making sandwiches; we were all occupied taking care of things. Rachel tried to go back in there, and Devin was right behind her to chase her back out, and he noticed that something was wrong. He called for my husband and me, knowing that something wasn't right, and took Rachel to the other end of the home.

My husband was the first one in the room, and coming right behind him, seeing that Zack was blue and didn't look like he was breathing, I immediately called 911, and they dispatched the ambulance while staying on the phone with me to give me instructions as to what we needed to do until they got there.

When the ambulance arrived, the EMTs were amazing and immediately took over; they handled it like professionals and were amazing. They loaded up into the ambulance, and my husband went with them. I remember telling Rachel and Devin that I loved them, calling Mike and my sister, and following the ambulance to the hospital. I'm not sure if that was the order everything happened in, but I do know that it all happened in a blur.

The rest of the night is full of moments of extreme clarity mixed with blurred and hazy times. I remember sitting outside the room in the emergency department waiting to hear him cry, waiting to hear someone tell me that he was going to be okay. They moved us to another room that was down the hall out of sight and earshot of the room he was in and asked us to wait for the doctor to come talk to us. I knew then, at that moment, that the outcome was bad. That moment was the exact point when I knew that my life as I had known it to be was never going to be the same again. I had this horrible feeling in the pit of my stomach; you can call it a hunch or instinct, whatever you want to call it…it wasn't good.

The doctor came in some time later and told us that they were unable to save him. My beautiful boy was pronounced dead by the medical staff at Community Hospitals and Wellness Centers in Bryan, Ohio, after all attempts to save his life had failed.

I sat there with my husband, Mike, and Heather, and I remember that my in-laws were there, my sister, and a few others. I honestly don't remember when everyone showed up. I was broken—mentally, physically, emotionally. I was numb and at the same time feeling emotions I didn't, and still don't, know how to fully explain.

They led us from waiting room to the trauma room where Mr. Man's body was. I didn't know what to do. My brain felt like it was shutting down, my heart felt like it was broken, my soul felt shattered, and I was falling apart. I don't think I was capable of processing much at that point. Others came in and out. Someone picked up Devin and Rachel and brought them up to the hospital, and we allowed Devin to be in the room, but I remember someone sitting in the waiting room with Rachel. We didn't want this to be part of her memory of Mr. Man.

At this point, I had clear moments of needing to call certain people and needing to handle the necessities, but some details are still blurred in my mind. I remember that the coroner came in along with the police to ask questions about the obvious: where was he, who found him, when was Zack last seen and by whom, any noises he made, and just a general interview.

I remember that all their questions just kept making my head throb. Their voices began to blur together like a swarm of bumblebees raging in my head. It was explained that this was a state requirement that an investigation be done because of Zack's age, and they needed information from our home as it was before anything else could be moved. I know that there were probably a million things they needed, and I just didn't have the wherewithal to comprehend it all. I remember our friend Sam being there, and he offered to take the officers to our home so that they could get the information that they needed.

That night was a blur of tears, anger, hurt, frustration, and countless other emotions I don't know how to describe. I felt like the heat of despair was meeting a frozen shell of grief and created the perfect storm inside my heart. They let us hold him, or Mr. Man's body at least. I knew that the body I was holding was not my Mr. Man anymore. This was the body of my youngest son, but this was no longer my Zackary. I felt his spirit leave. I heard the giggle echo around me as his spirit was completely free now, and he was on his way to the other side. I like to believe he was met by my mom, that he was greeted by the open arms of those who love him from the other side.

The hospital staff asked us what funeral home they should call, and we decided on the same funeral home that we used when my mom passed away. When the funeral director arrived, he gave us his card, and I remember that we set up a time to make arrangements. I am unsure if we set it up at that moment or if I called him the next morning. I know that we stayed there with Zack's body for as long as they would let us. I wasn't ready to leave, but we were finally given no choice. I think somewhere in the back of my mind, I thought if I stayed, never left, that everything would all be a horrible nightmare.

As we were walking through the corridors of the hospital toward the exit, some of the nurses and staff came out to see us. I had known some of them for quite a while, and I could tell by the looks on their faces they didn't know what to say or do. These professionals that are trained to handle these things were looking as lost as I felt. There was a lot of hugging; they told us how sorry they were and that we would be in their thoughts and prayers. I heard them, and I know they were sincere and meant what they said, but I wasn't really processing much at that point. I couldn't grasp everything, couldn't wrap my brain around everything. It was an overload of thoughts, emotions, and what everyone was saying.

To hear the words "I'm sorry about your son" was just not making it through the fog in my brain and soul. I was broken, too broken to be honest, to really grasp and understand their words and meaning. I was trying so hard to get a grip on just *existing* that I was merely going through the motions of acknowledging their words.

We left the hospital and went to the place we lived with Zack. I could not call it home at that point. We needed to pick up some things as we were going to stay with Mike and Heather for a while. I don't remember exactly how that was worked out; I just remember that it was. We also needed to shut some things off, change the answering machine, the quick cleanup type of things. I mostly just wanted to do these things to keep busy. I know that there were others that could have done it, but I needed to keep busy. I remember that I changed the answering machine to say that we had experienced a family tragedy.

We could not have been there for more than a few minutes when we got a phone call from the hospital. They wanted to know if we would be willing to donate any of Zack's organs. I couldn't do it. I know that sounds horrible, I know that the idea of saving someone else and that a part of him would live on is an amazing thing, but I could *not* let them do it. I knew that they were going to be performing an autopsy, but the thought of him being picked apart and pieces of him inside another person or even multiple persons shook me to my core even further. I could not come to terms with it. I'm sure there is a special place for me in regard to this, but I just knew that I would not have been able to handle it emotionally or mentally.

I remember calling a few family and friends while some of our things were getting packed up. I didn't know how long it was going to be before we would be able to stay there, or if it would ever happen. That point was when I realized that everything I had ever thought about the future since I found out I was pregnant with Zackary was no longer a possibility. Yes, some things would and could still happen because of Devin and Rachel, but it would no longer be the vision I had. There wouldn't be celebrations with all three of my children; there would now only be two. This just threw everything I knew into an upheaval, and I didn't know how to process it.

Every time I either called another family member or friend or they returned my call, and I had to tell them what had happened, my heart broke a little more. I didn't think that was possible, but it happened with each time I had to say the words "Zack passed away."

Who thought of those words as being the ones to represent someone's life ending? Those words, while sounding "nicer" than saying someone died, are almost harder to say. It puts you in limbo when you say that someone passed. I felt that I wasn't showing the full emotion I was feeling when I said those words. I felt that it didn't do justice to what my heart was feeling, the thoughts my brain was racing around my skull, or the mournful notes coming from my shattered soul.

That night as we left that house that we used to call home, everything felt surreal. I wondered if I was going to wake up from this horrible nightmare. That house was so empty without Zack's laugh and without his presence. We knew we were staying with Mike and Heather, but we had no idea for how long, and that was not a discussion I was capable of having. I am so thankful for everything they did to give us the time that we needed. For listening to us rant and rave and for loving our son just as much as we loved him ourselves.

The rest of the night is very hazy. I remember being up in the early hours of the morning because I wasn't able to sleep. Given today's technology, the use of the Internet was the unfortunate way that I notified a large number of people with as little repetition as possible. I don't remember getting any sleep until I passed out from total exhaustion later that day. I know my body needed the sleep, but it was just one more reminder that I was still here without Mr. Man.

I woke up thinking it was all a nightmare. I felt numb, like I really wasn't in my own body, hoping that what my brain was telling me was not real. Then I realized where I was at, and I knew that I really was living this horrible reality.

I remember waking up to a slew of things to do: phone calls, talking to people, crying, and feeling numb. I was so angry at everything that I could not see straight for hours. I remember staring at my other two children and being thankful that I still had them. I felt my husband's pain as it radiated off him in waves. We were not only drowning in our own grief, but I felt the grief from those around us like a tidal wave trying to suck us down farther into the depths.

All the people I loved and cared about were there with us at some point, sharing in our anguish and torture just as they had shared in our love and joy when Mr. Man was born. I felt adrift in an ocean of tears, anger, and turmoil—all the feelings I could feel personally and then compounded by the waves of those same feelings coming from my friends and family. I felt like I was in a tiny child's pool raft in the middle of the ocean during a tsunami. I felt worse because I could not fix their hurt. I could only watch it tear them apart inside, as my hurt was doing to me. I know that to me, it felt as though my heart was being ripped to shreds and my soul was being shattered by a sledgehammer, so I could only imagine that it felt the same for them.

My friends and family were akin to zombies, each of us merely going through the motions of our day because I can't believe that a single one of us actually knew what to do. I know that everyone wanted to comfort me, yet no one knew what to say. I wanted to comfort all of them, but I just felt numb, inside and out. Each of us was trying to wrap our thoughts around what had happened to us, and now we had to figure out how we were going to move forward from this moment.

Yes, I as Zack's mommy just lost my child, but my family was so close that when one of us was hurting, we all hurt. This was my son, I gave birth to him, but he was everyone's pride and joy. To say we all were in a state of shock would be an understatement. Most of us were walking around looking like the zombie apocalypse had started. Sleep was a commodity that many of us were not getting, appetites were slim to none, and it was common to find any one of us just sitting and hugging another friend or family member, and many of us hugged one or more of the kids more frequently than we ever had before. The shock did not necessarily go away, but it was joined by the hurt, anger, grief, and sorrow as the numbness faded.

However, like a great family does, we stuck together because we knew that if we didn't, we would never make it through this. When we needed something from the store, Mike and Heather would take care of it. With Devin and Rachel, my sister or others would come forward and help out when they could be either taking them for a while or coming over and keeping them occupied so that we could have a few moments of peace to take care of other things.

I remember that Mike brought me coffee, a *lot* of coffee. I live on the stuff even now, and he was practically bringing it to me by the gallons. I also remember that Heather threatened to sit on me if I did not eat. I really do think she would have tackled me to the ground and force-fed me if I wouldn't have agreed to eat whatever it was she brought me. I know this happened several times, and it was not that I was trying to starve myself or something stupid; I just simply had no appetite. Those first few days, everything tasted like cardboard, nothing had flavor, and I was only eating to keep everyone, specifically Heather, at bay.

I know that my sister contacted our family friend Deb in regard to performing the funeral, and also to an old family friend Darlene about the cemetery plot next to our mom. Both women had no issues taking care of these things, not that I was expecting any issues. Darlene felt it would be fitting that Zackary be buried next to Mom; the grandma who never knew him on this earth now held him for us on the other side.

I didn't know much at that point, but I did know one thing: that as long as I could keep it together, we would make it. I am not trying to imply that I did not have any breakdowns, because I most certainly did, but I knew that by keeping my wits about me through everything, it would get us further on our path. It was hard; sometimes I felt like I was trying to scale a mountain with an elephant on my back, but I knew in the long run that it would be worth it. Family sticks together, regardless of the size, and I was determined and hoping to make that happen.

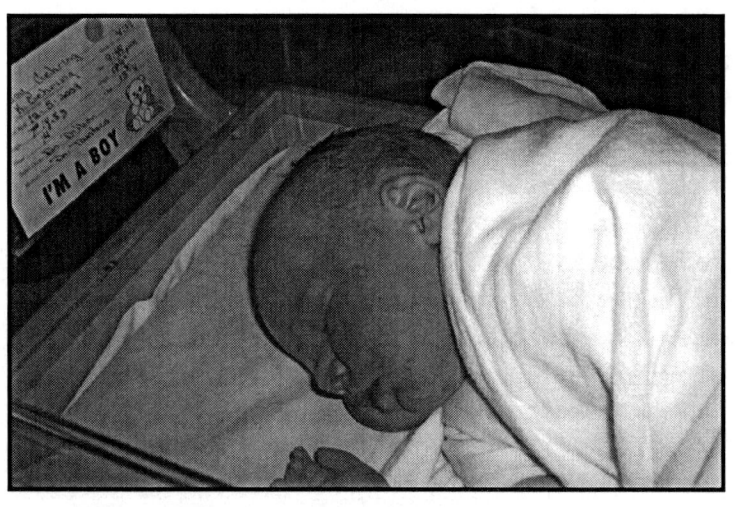

Zackary Allen "Mr. Man" Gehring—such a beautiful boy.

Mommy loving on Mr. Man.

5

THE HEALING BEGINS

Just about thirty-six hours after Zackary passed away, I felt the need to write, just write. I didn't care who saw it or really if anyone saw it. I didn't care what the words ended up being on the paper, just that I needed to get these thoughts out of my head onto something to ease up the pressure of all the emotions building up in my heart, soul, and mind. I chose to chronicle some of my thoughts on my Facebook account in the notes. I thought that this would be the easiest way to let my family and friends know what was going on in my heart.

That first journal entry, how I wrote it that day:

Zackary Allen Gehring 12/5/2009–5/11/2010

To my baby Zackary, my Mr. Man,

I wanted you before I knew you were you. I wanted you more the day I knew you were in my womb. The day we found out you were a boy is a day that still is strong in my mind because we finally knew that we could call you Zackary.

The day you were born was a miraculous day. Probably the only packed delivery room ever, it was standing room only, filled with your family that was waiting to welcome you into this world with open arms.

Your brother BEGGED for you, and the rest of us wanted you so badly that no words can explain. We loved you, cherished you, played with you, and thought we were so diligent in ensuring that you would be with us forever.

Unfortunately, for unforeseen reasons that none of us will ever understand, you have been taken from us. We all have a hole in our hearts that will never heal. We all feel empty because we can no longer hold you, kiss you, love you, and raise you in this large and loving family.

I still hear your laugh, see your smile, and I hope those memories never fade. Mommy and Daddy will never be the same without your smile and your love toward us. Your brother Dodo will never be the same without his baby brother, the one he asked for, the one he wanted to teach how to play baseball and play with Legos. Your sister Bug will never be the same as she gets older and realizes what she has missed. Your grandma will forever have a broken heart. Your aunts, uncles, and so many others that you graced with your love and your smile will never be the same after knowing you for so short a time and losing you for no reason that any of us can understand.

My Mr. Man—know that I always loved you, even before you were you, loved you with all my heart from moment one. Know that I will love you from now until eternity. If I could go back in time and fix this, I would. I would hold you in my arms and make sure that this horrible tragedy never happened, but alas, that is not within my power, and now I have to heal.

I have to take comfort in the thought that you are with your Grandma Kitti, Grandpa Chris, and numerous other family members that will take care of you until that day that I can hold you again in my arms, even though that will not be for a long time. I have your brother Devin and your sister Rachel that need me here.

But I still need you.

I love you, I miss you, and I always will.

Forever and always,

Love,
Mommy

I look back on those words, those emotions, and I wonder how on earth I was able to write *anything* at that time, let alone complete sentences that seem to me now to be so intense. I remember writing them, crying the whole time, and even now, crying again as I read over them for myself. I cry every time I read those words and other entries I made. The pain and tears will eventually ease, but will never go away. I have made a lot of progress on my path, but will have the rest of my life to travel down this road of healing. This is just the first step.

I remember just a few hours after writing this journal entry was when we had to go to the funeral home to make the final arrangements for Mr. Man's funeral. My *son's funeral.* The thought now still sends chills down my spine and makes me cringe. I hate that word to begin with simply because of the number of funerals I've attended, but to associate it with one of my children tore me apart.

When we set up the appointment, the funeral director told us to bring a few things for them to take care of Zackary. We had to bring whatever clothes we wanted him to be buried in and to make sure that we brought a hat because of the autopsy.

Bring a hat to cover his head after the autopsy.

We knew that Mr. Man was going to have an autopsy done, but it wasn't until they mentioned the hat that it really sunk in as to what they were going to be doing to *my baby boy*. We met with the funeral director, who was more than gracious to us by offering some of their services free to us, given the circumstances of losing our infant. We discussed options, chose the casket, and discussed the entire process that was about to occur. I had made funeral arrangements before, but this one was different. I knew what to expect, yet every step was hard, and every decision was harder.

The last time I made funeral arrangements, it was for my mother's funeral. I knew at some point I was going to have to do that, and then once she was diagnosed with cancer, I knew that those days were numbered. However, making funeral arrangements for your parent is something you *expect* to do at some point in your life; that is the natural order of things. Making funeral arrangements for my son, however, was not natural. I should not have had to do this. The funeral staff was very helpful, obviously seeing the toll that this had on us as a family. Each member of the staff that we encountered knew who our loved one was, and you could see the sorrow on their faces as a reflection of our own.

At the end of the meeting with the funeral director, I handed him everything we had brought for him to put on Mr. Man. As Zackary's mommy, there were just some things I needed to have done. I brought a blanket because he was still only five months old; he should be in a blanket, so that had to be done. We also brought a complete outfit of a one-piece undershirt and a sleeper because that is how I would have dressed him had he still been here with us. I also brought a diaper because his little behind should always be covered. That was the mommy in me still trying to take care of my baby in the only way I could or knew how to at that moment.

Finally, the hat that we brought was one that was bought for him by one of the aunts when I was still pregnant with him. This whole ensemble was part of the final acts for my baby, and I was going to make sure we did them right and make sure that he was dressed as I would have dressed him.

We left the funeral home knowing that our son was on his way back from having his autopsy in a local county that was larger than ours and more equipped for this. I could not help but feel that we were leaving everything behind again. Have you ever left somewhere and felt that you forgot something? That was my feeling. Deep in the core of my soul, I was not necessarily "forgetting" something; I was leaving something. The problem is that I knew exactly what, or better *who*, I was leaving behind.

We went back to Mike and Heather's, and I remember just sitting down and crying, then being angry, crying more, and then being numb. I felt like I should have been there at the funeral home when they brought him back. I felt the need to make sure that he was "okay." I know that sounds crazy considering that he was no longer alive. I just felt that as a mom, I should check those things. I wanted to be able to count his ten toes, his ten fingers, make sure that everything was how I knew it was supposed to be. How it was the very day he was born. I knew I would not want to see how he really looked after the autopsy, but I still had that urge to be there for him and with him.

I remember looking back at everything my family said about my journal posting. It was amazing to me how many people thought my words were beautiful and just how many people felt my hurt just by reading what I wrote. There were some friends that had not had the opportunity to spend much time with Mr. Man, but they felt their own grief because of my words. One of his aunts wrote, "I don't think there is anything more beautiful than you showing Zackary how much you love him, when he was here and now that he is gone!" Yet I felt I did not show enough.

Can you ever really show your love for someone "enough"?

Is that really possible?

I know that some things with some people can be on the verge of stalking, but that is not what I'm talking about. I am talking about when you honestly love someone, can you really show that love to them "too" much? Can we ever show our children "too much" love? Honest-to-goodness love, not the spoiling—the love.

You never realize how much love your heart can hold until you become a parent, and then you never realize how much pain you can feel until you lose your child. With that pain also comes the thoughts of what you should have done. I should have taken more pictures; we should have spent more time together as a family doing things, making extra special memories with pictures and stories to be able to share forever. But as they say, hindsight is better than foresight.

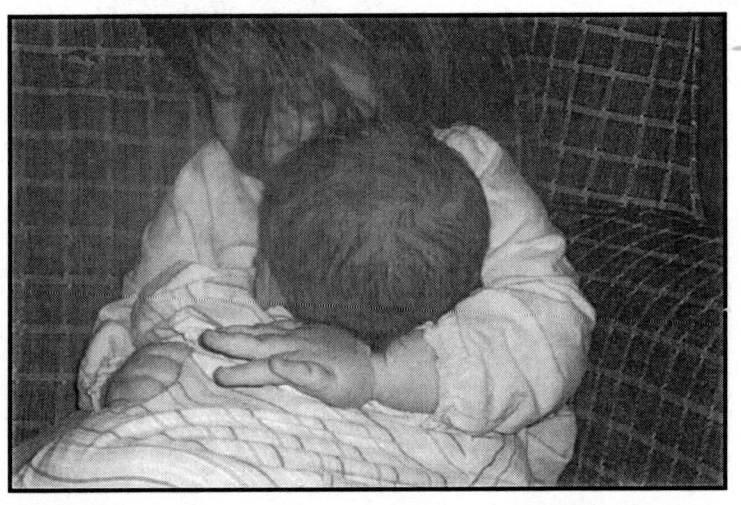

Little Miss Rachel trying to console Mr. Man; however,
she wouldn't need to console him if she would not have taken
his pacifier.

Rachel and Mr. Man. We would sit with Zack on the horseshoe pillow and talk with him and play with him. This time Rachel decided it was her time to play and snuggle with her little brother.

6

THE FLOOD OF EMOTIONS

Early Friday morning on May 14, just two and a half days after hearing the doctor tell me that she was sorry about my child's passing, my emotions went on their own little roller coaster.

This moment.

I'm sitting here, feeling guilty for having a migraine that won't quit, and I can't seem to get my brain to stop working about everything that has happened in the last few days.

I don't know if writing these things here is going to help or not—but I guess anything is worth a try.

Why? Why Zackary? Why me? Why my family?

Mr. Man was an absolutely wonderful baby boy—always happy, always smiling.

He was so loved by everyone who knew him even just a little bit, and he had all the women in his life wrapped around his little finger—Mommy included—but boy, his aunties, they had it bad.

All his aunts—all he had to do was make a little coo, and they would pick him up without hesitation. And yeah, Mommy was bad at that too.

Mr. Man had the rest of the family wrapped too—whether or not they want to admit it. Daddy was beside himself to be having another child, and to be having a boy was just the icing on the cake. And all the uncles—WOW—they were ready for him too.

And then there is Devin—he special ordered both his brother and sister in the order he wanted them, and he was wrapped around BOTH their fingers, even when he was frustrated because they were fussy. He would jump through hoops to make Mr. Man giggle and happy.

I sit here and wonder what he would have sounded like once he started talking, what he would have gotten into when he started to crawl (he was trying, but we only reached the inch-worm stage, regardless of how many times Daddy tried to show him how it was done).

I wonder how tall he would have gotten, the grades he would have gotten in school, what his favorite subject would have been (after recess, of course).

I wonder how the rest of his life would have played out had he just been given the opportunity.

Why wasn't he given the opportunity? Why weren't we given the opportunity to share these things with him?

Then I think about those women out there that get rid of their babies, give them up, don't take care of them, and wonder WHY they are allowed to continue to have these children, and I could not have mine.

Does that make sense? Does that seem fair? Why does my family have to hurt so much, and these women get to continue on with their lives by ruining others?

I feel bad when I cry, I feel bad when I don't cry, I feel bad when I can't seem to feel anything because I see the rest of my family hurting—and I can't fix it.

Even more messed up, I feel bad when I break down in front of everyone, yet when I am alone, I can't seem to feel anything but numb.

I know I am strong. I know I have to carry on for Devin and Rachel, but at the same time, part of me has died and will never come back.

May 11, 2010—my heart shattered, and no amount of super glue, epoxy, tape, etc., will ever put it back together the way it was. There will always be a piece missing. So how do I heal?

How do I learn to go on? How do I make the pain just a little less so I don't cry at the drop of a dime?

How do I help my family heal?

I love you, Zackary Allen "Mr. Man" Gehring—from moment one until the day I die and beyond. Wait for Mommy. And when my time is done here, when I have done my job with Rachel and Devin and the powers that be say it is time, I will come home to you. It's gonna be a long while because I've got a lot left to do here. I've got a lot left to finish before I can come home to you, so you stay with Grandma and Grandpa. They will guide you and love you until the day I can finally hold you in my arms again. I know for me it will seem like eternity until I see that sweet smile, but know that one day, Mommy will hug you once more.

And no, I do not wish to die. I am not suicidal, but I have realized that when my time comes and my time here on this plane is over, I will be sad to leave behind the ones that love me and that I love, but when my jobs here are done, my little boy is going to welcome me home with a smile, a giggle, and open arms, and knowing that…I will be at peace. That day may not be for another seventy years, but when that day comes, so too will my heart finally be healed.

There are those that talk about the "stages of grief"; some say there are seven, and I have even heard that there are twelve. Quite frankly, I don't care how many stages of grief there are. I will never be able to work through all of them to a point where I will finally be "through" the grieving process. There really is never a true "closure" on the grief of losing a child. This flood of emotions of anger, questioning, rage, and so many other emotions hit me like a ton of bricks exploding against a cement wall. I will never truly finish the grieving process because they all say that the final stage is acceptance, and regardless of how well I handle this journey, I will never accept the death of my son.

How I react has nothing to do with accepting it. I will be constructive in my life instead of destructive. I will work hard to keep his memory alive, but I will never accept that my child of five months had to die, with or without reason. How can I accept that a child who was perfectly healthy, was in a loving family who wanted him, begged for him, cared for him, and loved him, had to die? How can I accept all that knowing that this left us with nothing but questions, pain, grief, and holes in our hearts? How can I accept my son's death after seeing the world we live in today, knowing that there are those out there that do not deserve the life they have been given for whatever reason, and my son, who deserved the right to try to live, was taken? None of it made sense then, and it still doesn't make sense to this very day.

Then there are the emotions of the others around me going through this same flood. So many of those people we encountered during that first week after Zack passed tried, really tried, to give us words of encouragement, of support, and of wisdom. Yet for all their trying, most honestly failed. Some statements made me angry, and I had to bite my tongue to prevent from lashing out at what I felt was obvious stupidity.

I know that sounds rude, but there were some that focused on *their* beliefs and feelings, and when you base your statements on your feelings without considering the person you're talking to…well, that just isn't polite, and that would be the easiest way to put it. Some statements were pretty general: "I'm sorry about your son, someday you will be with him again." While others just got under my skin: "Jesus called him home, you should be rejoicing!"

Seriously? *That* is your comforting statement?

I really just had to walk away. My son *was* home. My son *was* where he belonged, in our arms. He did not belong anywhere else but at home with his mommy and family. I do not have that anymore, so nothing you can say will change that, but I most certainly will not be "rejoicing" anytime soon, or ever, about it. You can't sugarcoat it, and you making me feel like I just need to "rejoice" only makes me feel worse. I no longer have one of my children here with me, and for you to make it sound like this is a reason to party feels like rubbing salt into a huge wound.

I am sure that there are those that over time would rejoice in their loved one being "called home by Jesus." Not everyone has that feeling or belief. Not everyone will be able to look past the pain, hurt, and grief to see the joy that you see in that. Let's also take this situation just as one instance—my child just *died*. Why would you tell me to rejoice?

I understand that those individuals that said those things meant well, I really do. However, I do not think that they really thought about what they were saying and how it might have been perceived at that time. I know that no one knew what to say to me or my family; we did not know what to say to them either. This almost made me feel like I should be "happy" because of how *they* viewed it. I know that probably isn't what they meant, and I'm sure that they were trying to console me. With everything that was going on at that time—the level of grief I was trying to cope with and the fact that my brain was not firing on all cylinders—my ability to process everything was limited.

I wanted to scream from the mountaintops that this was not right. I wanted to find those young moms out there that did not want their children and gave them up to shake the mothers senseless. I wanted to curl up into a ball and cry until I had no more tears left and then cry some more. Yet none of these things would change what happened. This was my turning point.

I don't believe that things happen without a reason. I do not have to agree with the reason or purpose, nor do I have to like it. However, I *do* have to learn from it, grow from it, and take that experience internally and decipher what it means to me. I needed to find some sort of peace, but I wasn't sure how. I just knew that I needed to keep in the forefront of my mind that my son's death was for a reason that was much bigger than I could comprehend, and I needed to hold on to that. In a way, this thought stabilized me just enough to give me that little twinkle of peace that I needed. That is all I needed to start with because I knew that the little twinkle of peace would plant itself like a seed deep inside of me and begin to grow. I knew that it was going to take time, that I was going to have to work on it and nurture that seed, but I was determined to stay the course. I knew that in order for us to survive and for me to be able to take care of my other two children properly, I was going to need patience, my survival instincts intact, and a lot of faith in myself.

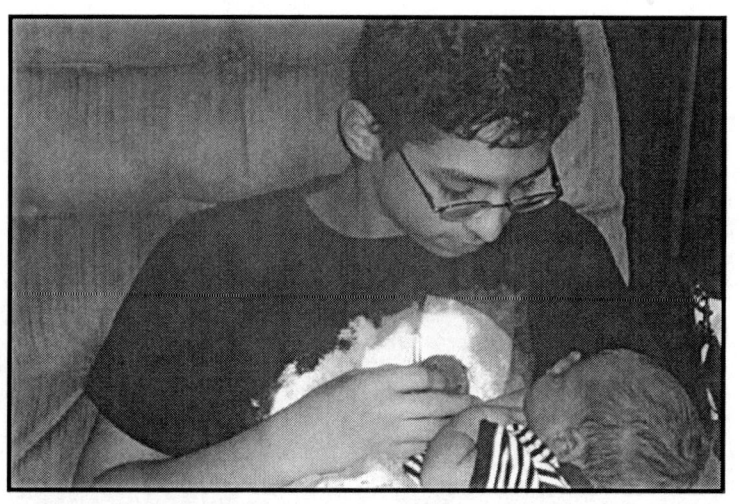
Devin and Zackary. You can see that he is just enthralled by having a baby brother and proud as can be too.

7

THE SHOWING

Arrangements made, family and friends notified, and it was time. I was not ready for that "time" to get here, but it came anyway. It was time to go to the funeral home for the showing. I think the most common statement out of my mouth that morning was "Dammit, I can*not* do this." I somehow managed to pull it together on the outside, but inside I was a wreck.

We arrived and knew that things were going to be crazy, but I was determined to make this a celebration of the time that we had with Zackary. I had been to my fair share of funerals in my life. Coming from a large family, it was inevitable, and I had experienced every aspect of a funeral that you can imagine. Family fights, panic and anxiety attacks, reminiscing, crying, laughing at family stories, and even total silence. I knew that I wanted to share with everyone the joy that Mr. Man brought to us, and that was a monumental task.

I walked into the funeral home, and I knew every room. This was the same funeral home where we had my mother's funeral. I also knew, before walking through the doors, exactly where the location of my baby's casket would be. That was an eerie realization—my *baby's* casket. I took a deep breath and kept walking. I had to do this, and I had this thought of *I'll be damned if fear will stop me from saying my final good-byes.*

You reach a moment where you are stuck between a rock and a hard place. You don't *want* to do it, but you know you *need* to do it. The thought of this being a "final" good-bye caused me to mentally blank out. I don't know why those were the words I thought at that exact moment because they just made the whole situation more chaotic in my mind, but I knew I had to deal with it and hold it together long enough to get through this.

As I approached the casket, a lump formed in my throat, the dam broke, and the sobs came. I took those final steps and *touched* that box, and at that moment, that was all I could consider it, a box—and I felt cold from the top of my head to the tips of my toes. It wholeheartedly felt like I had been doused with a bucket of ice water. I knew what I was touching; I knew that this was forever where Mr. Man's body would be held. My hands were shaking as I reached out, and I touched Zack's hand, his face, and then put my hand on his stomach. I knew he was not there anymore, but that was still his body.

I won't even begin to sugarcoat it. I wanted to scream, cuss, cry, and know *why*! Dammit! He was wanted, loved, and cherished! This is not the natural order of things! I am not supposed to outlive my child! My *three* children were supposed to be the ones to bury me after a long life, when I was old, gray, decrepit, and most likely insane. My *three* children were supposed to be able to hold each other and be there for each other after I took my last breath. This was *not* how it was supposed to be. I was not supposed to be comforting two of my children after the death of their baby brother.

I struggled with that every moment at that point; how do you help a twelve-year-old and a two-year-old understand that people who are not sick can die for no reason? How do you help them understand that people can die just "because" and not due to an accident? How do you help your children understand things you yourself, as an adult, can't comprehend?

I felt my family get closer to me, and I knew that I had to hold it together, if nothing else, for them. I knew that for us to make it through this, we had to try to do it together. While I will agree that they needed to see me have my emotions, I needed to not completely fall apart. We hugged as a family, and I knew then that in some way, shape, or form, we were going to all survive. I didn't know what the outcome was or the how, but I knew that one way or another, we will pull through this because we are survivors.

Devin was still walking around in a daze. I had no idea how I was going to help him through this. One moment he would look okay, and the next he would be sitting somewhere crying silently. I watched him closely as he went up to the casket; he grabbed my hand and placed his other hand on Mr. Man's hand. My heart was already broken, but as I watched my oldest child let go and sob uncontrollably from that much emotional pain, my heart broke even more.

Emotional pain is not something that you can heal with a Band-Aid and a kiss. I did not know how to help him deal with his emotions because I was still trying to learn how to deal with my own. I did what I knew. I pulled him close to me, and he hugged me as tight as he could while crying. Daddy picked Rachel up and brought her over to the casket. Rachel put her hand out to touch Zack and stopped just short of actually touching his hand. She seemed to be unsure if she wanted to touch him, and we didn't want to force it. We told her that it was okay, and instead she put her hand out to reach for Dodo. Devin took her in his arms, and they went off to the other side of the room and sat down. I stood there in silence with my husband for some time. I have no idea as to how long it really was. It was as if time stood still.

Family and friends started showing up soon after, and it was time to "put on my game face," as I called it. I needed to help them just as much as I needed to help myself. I needed to let them know that I was a survivor. Some of the family members had never seen Zack; others had only seen him once or twice. Then there were others that had seen him almost every day of his life. Each person that came in I talked with, hugged, cried with, and felt their sorrow as much as my own. That was the hardest part. I had my own grief and sorrow, and I could feel those same feelings from each and every person I was near that day. That made things harder. I am usually the one to "fix" things, and this, no matter how much I wanted to, I could not fix.

There were some family members that brought food to the funeral home, others brought things to drink, and some gave us cards with different things in them. Each family member was doing their best to hold it together however they knew how. I felt like a lost pinball for a while, bouncing around from family member to friend and back to family. I never really had a "place" that I stayed for very long. I felt very high-strung, and I did not want to snap like a rubber band, so I kept moving. At one point, one of the cousins nailed me down and told me I needed to eat, even making the sandwich for me. I remember as I sat there and ate that I watched other family members interact with each other.

Some family and friends were very somber; others joked about how Mr. Man would giggle at anything and everything. For each person there, the experience was theirs—and mine. I dealt with the usual "comfort" remarks, and I just thanked the individuals and kept trucking along. I knew that they meant only to comfort me, but you can only hear so many "He's gone home" before you start to feel a little more insane than when you started the day. I still felt like I was on a horror-themed roller-coaster ride. I did not want to relax, I did not know what to do with myself as the showing came to a close, and I sure as hell did not want to leave.

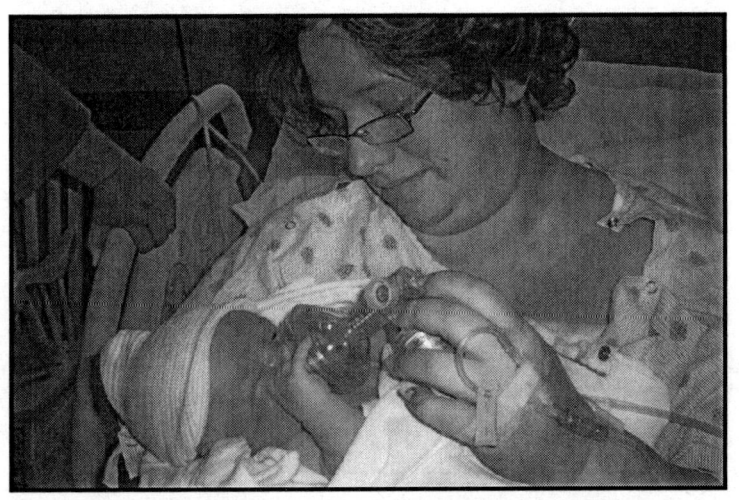

Mommy and Mr. Man. I didn't care how I looked,
I was just so happy to finally have this little
bundle in my arms instead of my belly.

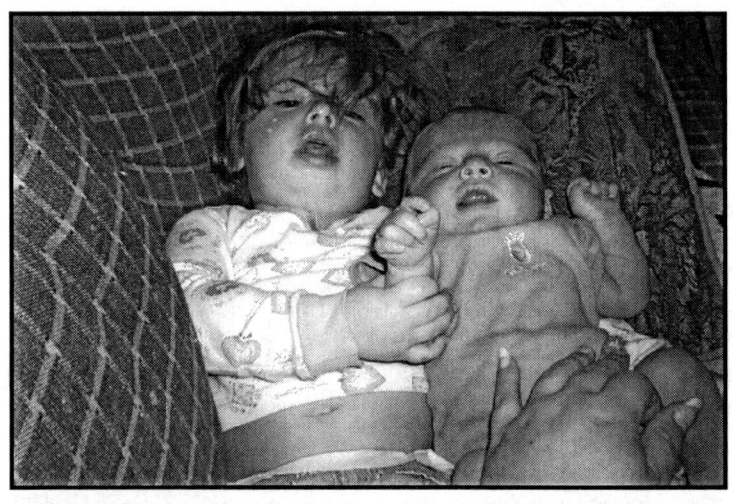

Rachel and Mr. Man. She was so determined to be a part of everything he did and to be able to help with everything he needed. It is hard to realize that her memories of him are not many.

8

AFTER THE SHOWING

At the end of the evening, we were allowed time to hold Mr. Man one last time before the funeral and then burial. Think about that—*one last time.* That thought just hits you right in the gut when you realize what that really means.

We met with the funeral director outside of the room where Zack's casket sat. We listened to the director explain to us how it would feel to hold him, how it won't be like it was when he was alive, the purpose of the hat, and so on.

I knew that holding him would be different. My son's body was no longer alive. I knew that it would feel different not having him snuggle into me. I knew that he would no longer reach for me. I knew that he wouldn't wiggle around to get his head into the crook of my neck just under my chin. I knew that I wouldn't hear him coo and giggle, and

I wouldn't hear him make little grunting sounds as he was trying to get comfortable. I knew that I would no longer be able to pat his butt to put him to sleep. I knew that I wouldn't be able to kiss his forehead and hear him giggle afterward. I knew that I would never again give him a raspberry on his chubby little cheeks and make him giggle before he settled down into snuggling with Mommy.

I knew all of these things, but it didn't stop me from wanting to hold him again. I don't regret for one moment wanting to hold him again. I remember my thoughts at that moment in time that I just wanted him back in my arms. I didn't worry about what was different. I didn't worry about what wasn't "right." I just wanted what to me was all I had left, and that was holding my son in my arms again. *One. Last. Time.*

I remember the funeral director saying, "His body won't feel the same as you remember. He will feel stiff, and that is because of the embalming process." *Wow.* That was my only thought when he said that. I give the funeral director credit for being able to say that to a grieving mother without stumbling over his words once with a total sober look on his face.

He then continued to tell us more information. "You have to be careful how you move him, don't bump him into anything." My sarcastic side wanted to come out, but I held it at bay. I mean, really? I wouldn't have bumped him into anything when he was still alive, why would I do it now? I know that he was only telling us what he was supposed to say, but it just grated under my skin. I can admit to having that feeling, and I can also say that I had enough wits about me to just keep my mouth shut and listen to his instructions.

The funeral director continued with, "Please remember that after the autopsy, he also has plastic under his clothing to prevent any issues." That part bothered me on a molecular level. I knew what he meant and did not want to explicitly state. I knew that he meant well and wanted me to understand what I was going to be dealing with. I still think that they need to try to find different ways to explain things to grieving family members. I am not saying he did a bad job, but the delivery felt *too* practiced, almost canned. I do not envy his job, but at that point it would have been nice to see some emotion from him when you take into consideration the things he was saying to us.

I sat down in a chair that had been moved closer to Mr. Man's casket, and the funeral director lifted Zack's body from the casket and placed him in my arms. The weirdest feeling of peace overcame me at that point, if only for a moment, of having Zackary back in my arms. I knew then at that moment why some parents totally lose their minds after the death of a child. This was a hellacious roller-coaster ride of emotions that I had been on. I can easily see why some parents don't know which end is up and why families fall apart. If you don't know how to handle your own emotions, how can you communicate those feelings or even deal with them? There is a huge difference from dealing with and handling emotions, and if you can't do both in a traumatic moment like this is for a parent, you begin to lose yourself. That is a slippery slope to be on. When you start to lose yourself, it's not only hard to regain footing to stop the slide, it is even harder to try to get back to where you were.

I asked the funeral director to remove the hat from Mr. Man's head, and he slightly freaked out. He wanted *nothing* to do with that. "Mrs. Gehring, I do *not* think you understand fully why the hat is there, and I *really* do not think you want to see that."

I, however, made it abundantly clear that the hat was coming off, one way or another. Yes, I know that my son had an autopsy performed. Yes, I know to some extent as to what that entailed. Yes, I know that *logically*, I probably should not see it.

Yes, I do believe that I am insane.

After much convincing, the funeral director did take off Zack's hat. Truth be told, seeing the scars from his autopsy did not freak me out like I think he was expecting. I knew about it, was prepared for it, and I just had to know. I guess in some ways I needed to see that to know that this was not really the most horrible nightmare I had ever experienced.

I *had to know* that this was, in fact, my reality. Then, as I was looking at Zack, trying to make sure I memorized every inch of his face, it was at that moment that I realized that I never had cut his hair.

As trivial as it is, I freaked out, but only a little. My anxiety about everything I would never do with Mr. Man kicked up a notch. It wasn't like I started screaming or outwardly freaking out; it was just simply an inner emotional reaction. I realized that I *had* to have some of his hair. I had hair from my other two children, I *needed* some of his just as much. I knew that this was not only the last time I would have this chance, but this might also be the only opportunity I might have to make this happen. I would never have another chance to cut his hair, straighten it, comb it, push his hair out of his eyes...never again have any of these chances.

I spoke to the funeral director and asked him to get me a pair of scissors and a comb. To say that he wasn't keen about it was probably an understatement. I know that considering the situation, he probably expected hysteria when the hat came off. With this request being my reaction, I'm sure he wasn't prepared for that. He looked slightly shell-shocked, and I suspect he thought I finally stepped off the deep end. I was, and still am, Zackary's mommy. I am the one that should give him his first haircut as I did for my other two children.

The funeral director tried to dissuade me, suggesting that I not put myself through that kind of emotional trauma. He staunchly stated that he did not think this was a good idea. I did not agree with him.

After much convincing, the funeral director finally brought me a pair of scissors, a comb, and a small pouch to place the hair in. With the funeral director poised to catch the hair trimmings, I gave my son his first, last, and only haircut as his daddy held him. Mr. Man's hair was so fine and soft, unlike his siblings. Both of my other children had very thick hair, and Devin's was always very coarse. Mr. Man's hair being so fine was such a contrast in feeling and touch that I won't ever forget that for so many reasons. I had to be careful as I was combing his hair for obvious reasons, but it was so amazing for me to be able to do this one simple gesture. At that one brief moment, I felt peace. For that *one moment*, I was able to just be Zack's mommy, doing what I was supposed to do. I didn't have to worry about what was going on around me. I was focused on what I was doing, not the scar, not where we were, just focused on cutting my baby's hair.

I know that to someone who is not an Angel Parent that this seems morbid, odd, possibly insane; yet the fact that I was able to do this one thing for my baby boy that I had done with my other two children made me feel better.

That feeling may have been fleeting, lasting only a few brief moments, but it was there nonetheless.

That moment in time was therapeutic to a small extent. This was, in all honesty, the *last thing* I was ever going to be able to do for him as his mommy. I could not fix this. No amount of kisses and Band-Aids would change the situation we were in, what happened to my baby boy, or what was happening to my family.

I think back to that moment, and I know that to anyone else watching, it would have been the strangest sight—a grieving mother cutting the hair of her child who had passed away and who will be buried the next day. To me, it was another way for me to have that mother-child connection with my youngest son. There are things I knew I would never get to do with him, so I was taking advantage of the things that I *could* do, right up to the very last moment.

That night once we got back to Mike and Heather's and after we got the kids settled down and in bed, I wrote this:

> *Today starts a new beginning*
> > *Today starts a healing*
> > *Today starts a soul-searching*
> > *Today starts a different chapter in my life*
> > *Today starts a spiritual searching*
> > *Today starts a spiritual healing*

Today was the showing for my son Zackary

Surrounded by friends and family today and seeing how many people love and care for me and my family was a bit of an eye-opener. Today was not about a life full of memories, years of experiences, multiple achievements, but a life cut short at five months and six days.

So today those people were not there just because they loved my son, but because they loved my family in some way, be it friend, family, or friends that might as well be family.

And in the midst of all this—I still have peace. The peace that my son, even though he should be in my arms, and it is not right that I bury him, he is in the arms of my mother, his grandma, and the arms of my father-in-law that I never had the opportunity to know, his grandpa.

I have peace in the fact that I was given a gift of five months—five joyous loving months. I have peace in the fact that my family will make it through this somehow, standing tall like my son would expect us to.

The other day I was listening to music while driving—as I always do—and a song came on that I would NEVER thought would apply to what we are going through, but there were parts to it that just spoke to not only my heart, but my soul. Once again, it gave me peace, and it gave things meaning for me. The song is "I'm Yours" by Jason Mraz.

After listening to this song, I realized that I have let so many things pass me by because I felt that I would always have the time for them, that everyone I knew, knew how I felt about them, or whatever procrastination I felt suited the situation and that I needed to stop it.

I have been given so many gifts in life that I thought I had cherished enough, and now, I am not really sure that I did. My family is a gift to me, my mother, my sister, they are all gifts that I never cherished enough, and now with my sister, I don't tell her enough.

My oldest son, Devin, is a definite gift to me. He is part of the reason I am who I am today. He gave me joy when I felt that I had nothing to be happy about, especially when my marriage to his father was failing. He got me through all the rough times just by being himself and loving his mommy.

Rachel is also a gift. She keeps me laughing when I don't think I can laugh anymore. She has such a beautiful smile that there are days I believe that the sun cannot shine until she smiles because the sunshine comes directly from that smile.

Precious Zackary—a blessed little gift. My Mr. Man that was always smiling and happy. Even when he was *crabby, he would still smile. He had a way of making you forget all your troubles, regardless of what they were.*

Then there are others in my family—Heather and Mike, Opal and Dave, Heather and Ryan, and the list goes on of people I have relied on so much for input, advice, love, friendship, family, and fun. They all are gifts to me in their own individual ways. Without them we would be lost because they individually give us something that no other person can or could.

That brings me to now, this moment, today—all my gifts have been presented to me in a way today on an emotional level that I am not sure I can express in any type of words, but to each gift I love separately, individually, and with a whole heart. Those that were there with me today and held my hand said they thought I was strong made me feel that way. Those that were not there were there in spirit and made me understand in a spiritual way that I am loved regardless of the circumstance and regardless of the distance.

Everything today made me realize that I am strong. I am a woman, a mother, a friend, a sister, a daughter, a niece, a cousin, and many other hats I can't begin to list. I am a momma bear that must take care of her cubs.

But I am also grieving, hurting, in pain, and missing part of my heart.

BUT I am also a woman, a mother, a friend, a sister, a daughter, a niece, a cousin, and all those other hats, and a momma bear that must let my cubs take control for the first time in my life.

And for once, I think I am okay with that. For once I think I understand why I have been given all these gifts, so that for all those that I have touched out there in some way, be it through my love, my help, my friendship, or whatever way I have touched their hearts, that they were given to me to be MY support because in the end, I have realized that maybe I was given as a gift to them for the same reason.

And believe it or not, that is not only a humbling experience, but it's liberating. It is freeing to know that I am not on this earth to just go through the motions. I am not just here to be a stick in the mud or a blob on a log, but to achieve something. And I personally feel that that achievement is to be me to those that love me and let them be themselves to me—one of the many that loves them back.

So this is a thank-you to all of you I love—my family, my children Devin, Rachel, and Zackary, Kara, Dave, Damian, Angel, Heather, Mike, Heather, Ryan, Dave, Opal, Jade, and the numerous others that I can't begin to thank, list, etc.

But most of all, my love goes mostly to my children. For dealing with me, loving me, accepting me, and in the end, never letting me forget that they love me just as much. And thank you for guiding me down my path, for all of you alone have given me a reason to do the things I do and pushing me to be a better person, a more confident person, and just all around helping me be me.

For those of you who read this, thank you for listening to the rambling...that alone means more than you know.

This was a turning point for me, the timeframe when I wrote that piece. I was not quite sure where to take it at that time, but it was a turning point nonetheless. I knew that at that very point, while my heart and soul were shattered and I was broken emotionally, that I would survive. I knew that no matter what happened, from that moment on, I would definitely make it. I *had* to make it. I knew that nothing I did could "fix" or change what happened to Mr. Man, and I knew in the depths of my heart and soul that I would see him again. With this realization, it was like flipping a light switch to the on position and the alarm clock going off all at the same time.

I remember that "I've had an epiphany" feeling that night. I remember sitting in front of the computer, knowing I needed to get things out of my brain and onto paper, the journal, something…*anything*. I knew that things were starting to make sense with how I needed to begin handling my emotions; they were starting to click into place and starting to come together. On the other hand, I knew it was going to take a lifetime before I would *fully* understand it all. I knew that this was going to be a journey that I would not only take with those of my friends and family beside me, but also there would be times that I would walk parts of the journey alone.

That night, I felt that I was being shown something. I'm not sure if that something was a light to the path, an arrow, but it was something. I do not believe in coincidences, and nothing happens without reason. Now that I was given a direction, it was my job to follow it and start to rebuild, to be constructive, and to start to live my life in a way that would not only keep Zack's memory, but also show my other two children that even when tragedy strikes, it does not stop the world from turning.

Now to just really do it. That was going to be the most interesting part of it all. I knew what I needed to do, but the question was *how* to do it. The next question would be did I feel that I had the strength to get it done? I wasn't sure, but I was going to give it my all. I knew that it was not going to be easy, and the first step would be to get through the funeral and to mourn for my son who left us too soon.

Devin and Rachel. She was just a little bit, and this is one of my favorite pictures of these two.

9

THE FUNERAL

The day of Zack's funeral was just a dreary day. Being the middle of May, one would not have expected it to be as chilly as it was, but it was overcast, dreary, chilly, and rain was in the forecast. Mother Nature was mirroring my emotions that day, and I took it as a sign that the universe was mourning with me and mourning *for* me. In a way, it gave me comfort that it seemed as if the whole universe was hurting with me, that it wasn't just me.

As we were all getting ready for the funeral, I did a last-minute changeup. As I have said, I am simple, and my kids have been raised simple and just down-to-earth type people. I decided that we were going to give Zack his final good-byes *our* way—jeans, T-shirts, and boots if you had them. I called everyone in the family that I could in the short time given and told them the change of plans. We finished getting around and left for the funeral home.

Once people started arriving, it really started hitting home as to what we were all there to do. Everyone there physically, mentally, and emotionally were there to say *good-bye* to my son, Zackary. This realization hit me hard, and I faltered a bit in my strength. It was hard to comprehend that this was *the last time* I was ever going to see Zack's physical body.

I went off away from everyone and just took a moment to find some semblance of peace. I had to. I did not have a choice to make the world stop spinning because my heart was broken and I felt shattered. I did not have the ability to go back in time and change the events that led up to that moment in time. So I found a way to reach deep down and pull up every ounce of strength I could find. That was hard, and there was not much there to pull up at that moment.

As I watched the chairs fill up with family and friends, I saw faces that I had not seen in years, ones that I had not been able to stay in touch with simply because life gets in the way. It really is true that you see most of the people you know at two moments in your life: weddings and funerals. There were faces that, over the course of the showing and funeral, I had only known distantly through other family members or friends. They were there to show their support to us and to our family because it affected them just as much. I took comfort in knowing that so many just wanted to be there. Even if none of them knew what to say, them being there was more than I could have really asked for.

That is what so many people do not understand about things when this type of tragedy hits. The parents don't *need* you to say anything. What they need is that shoulder and that knowledge that when they feel that they are about fall over, you will be there to help hold them up. They need to know that no matter what, you still love them in some fashion.

Grieving parents do not need to hear "I'm sorry" or "Are you okay?" Grieving parents need some form of normalcy. That was all I hoped for at that point. I needed my friends and family to remember that my son was and always will be a part of me, regardless of their personal beliefs, as that was how I believed. I needed everyone there to take a memory with them, no matter how small, of my son. I needed that seed to be planted in as many minds as possible because by more people remembering him, he truly is never gone. I needed that seed to grow into something beautiful, a blossom full of memories of a beautiful soul that left this world far too soon.

Once again, I felt the need to roam; I couldn't sit still for very long. I greeted everyone as they arrived, friends, family, acquaintances; each person that came in I felt the need to acknowledge that they were there and to thank them. It amazed me as to how many people were there. This funeral was for my five-month-old little boy, a child who touched so many lives just by *being alive*. Here all these people were to mourn the loss of this light from this world. It just really hit home as to how much one person can do by just being who they are. Zackary lived five short months and managed to give pure love to all these people in one way, shape, or form, and they were all there to acknowledge that. They were all here to say their good-byes and to mourn with each other. It was simply amazing to me.

The funeral started just as most funerals do. Deb Campbell officiated for the funeral, just like she did my mother's. Words were spoken about the love, the family, and the pain of the loss. I can't tell you specifics because I had reached a point that I was running on pure adrenaline, and my brain just was not together because of trying to get through everything. I wasn't numb, but I had reached a point of sensory overload with everyone that was there and everything that was going on. I was listening, but it wasn't sinking in, and my brain felt jumbled. I was too busy watching my family and, of course, staring at that small casket in front of me.

At one point, Opal broke down hard. This was a lot for anyone to deal with, but Opal and her family had been a constant through my entire pregnancy with Zack; she used to call him ZigZag because of his initials. She adored him

I think almost as much as I did. I couldn't just let her be. I went to her. Yes, in the middle of my son's funeral, I went to console his aunt. I know, I have been told numerous and countless times how very odd I am.

That is how this group was—when one hurt, we all hurt. At the same time, knowing that she loved *my* son so much to be hurting this badly, it was the right thing for me to do…go to her side. Deb paused the funeral while I was sitting there with Opal, knowing that to me, the words could wait, but Opal could not. I knelt in front of her, holding her as best as I could and told her that we were going to get through this. I remember the look in her eyes of indescribable pain. I knew that nothing I did could help or fix that pain, but I held her as close as I could. I let her know, without a word being said, that we would do this together.

I returned to my seat once Opal had calmed down a little, and Deb then continued with the funeral. I know at one point I spoke about how much joy Zackary brought to my life. I talked about the little song I sang to him. Other than that brief moment, the rest of the funeral went by in a blur of words and faces.

We went through the final processional of friends and family saying their final good-byes to Zackary and of course showing their support to us. There were some that simply walked past the casket and came to us and hugged each of us. Others stood there at the casket and stared at him, touched him, and said how much they loved him and would miss him.

Each and every person that was there came by and hugged us, and some did not want to let me go. The love and the hurt in that room at that very moment was tangible. You could feel in the air and in every ounce of your being. I felt like I was surrounded by a maelstrom of love and pain. I remember this moment almost like watching a movie. I was there, but yet I *wasn't*. Physically I went through all the motions, but emotionally and mentally, I felt like I was outside of my body, watching this whole scene play out. I was partially numb, partially on sensory overload, and I did not know how to process it all. I was left with nothing else but to go with the flow of things. I talked to each person, hugged, shook hands, and all the while feeling out of sorts.

I stood and noticed all the things that were left in the casket with Mr. Man. I know that I put my senior key from high school along with my mom's senior key from high school in there. I also know that his father placed items, Devin put in a sweatshirt and a toy car, and there were several others that placed a cherished item in there as well. There were photos from several individuals, a hat from Uncle Sam, and trinkets from other loved ones. I know that we ended up having to go to a larger-sized casket because of all the things that were placed in with him.

I stood there with my husband and the pallbearers as we were all the last ones to leave the room where Zack's casket was located. I stood in the foyer of the funeral home watching everyone gather their things and group together to walk out. Everyone was filing out of the funeral home to get into their vehicles for the processional to the cemetery. I looked back into the room where the pallbearers were gathered, and I saw that Zack's casket was closed. The funeral director must have closed it as soon as we walked out of the room. I knew that there was still a cover to be placed on it to finish sealing it, but I didn't want to watch that. One of the staff came over to see if I needed anything and offered to help me get into the limo with Rachel, and I just let him lead the way.

The funeral home arranged for the four of us to ride in the family vehicle that they have available, which just happened to be a limo. Oddly enough, this was my first time ever riding in a limo. It was strange to realize that I was finally getting to do something I had always wanted to do, but this was *not* how I wanted to do it. I helped Rachel into the limo and turned to look back at the funeral home. I knew at any point that the pallbearers were going to be bringing out the casket to load it into the hearse in front of the limo.

This was it.

Never again was I going to see my baby in the physical sense.

Rachel reached out and grabbed my hand, and I smiled at her as I squeezed her hand back with my own. She knew that things weren't right, and she knew that her baby brother was not here anymore. The problem was that at this age, she did not understand. That was the problem for me at that time because I did not know how to help her understand that which I did not understand myself. I buckled her into her car seat that someone had already loaded in and buckled down. Devin and my husband joined us in the limo after the hearse was loaded with my baby's casket. The driver let us know that he was set to go, and then the processional to the cemetery began.

At this point, I knew I had time to think because the ride from the funeral home in Bryan, Ohio, to the cemetery was about a thirty-minute drive. Zackary was going to be buried in Tedrow Cemetery just north of Wauseon, Ohio. He was buried next to my mother. Tedrow is a little blip on the map of northwest Ohio, and it is where I had some of my best memories from my childhood. My mom's best friend, Darlene, grew up there, and we spent a lot of time with her and her family as I was growing up. Darlene was the one who purchased the two plots originally when my mother passed away in 2003, and the plot is right with all of her family's plots. To me it was very fitting because as a child, I did not know any different than Darlene and her family being my family too.

When Zack passed away, Darlene offered up this plot for us to use, and to be honest, I could not imagine a better place for his final burial than to be right next to his grandmother. At the time of Zack's passing, I had not yet been able to get a headstone for my mother, and it almost felt like this was the reason. Once again, it came back to the fact that I don't believe in coincidences. Each thing that has happened to me has happened for a reason. Every step in my life has had a connection to something else in the future. Be it from the free will of others or my own, everything is connected in some way.

The drive to the cemetery was filled with talking to Rachel and keeping her occupied on the ride. I would point out things of interest on the side of the road. "Rachel, look at the horsey!" Any animal we would pass we would mention, and it kept her from fidgeting too much. Other than what was said to Rachel, the rest of us were pretty silent. What do you talk about at that point? What is there to say when your first ride in a limo is to take your son's casket to a cemetery? I think I might have actually said something like, "Well, now I know what it's like to ride in a limo." That was probably the extent of any conversation outside of talking to Rachel.

I would occasionally look back to see the processional of vehicles that were following us, and I was amazed at every turn by just how many vehicles there were.

Upon arriving at the cemetery, it was a *harsh* reality check. I knew why we were there; I had been down this road before when my mother passed away, and now...now this was for my *baby boy*. That moment in time could only be described as hell. I knew that every inch farther into the cemetery was one more step closer to the ultimate final good-bye to Mr. Man.

Once we stopped, we all filed out of the limo, and we were joined by our family and friends to follow us. We had a processional of friends and family following behind us as we followed the pallbearers carrying Zack's casket up to the location of his final resting place. That is a really hard sentence to say when speaking of your child. This was *his final resting place*.

Forever.

Never again would I rock him to sleep. Never again would he curl up beside me and giggle. Never again would I see him cradled in the arms of his father, brother, or other family members. Never again would I yell at his aunts for coddling him because he made a little noise. Never again would I see all three of my children playing together. I would never have the chance to yell at the boys for being mean to their sister. I would never have the chance to yell at Rachel for invading her brothers' rooms.

It began to crash into me like a tidal wave that wasn't stopping. I had to stop my thoughts from raging on before they got the better of me. Even now, writing these words when years have passed since this day, I have to pause. I can remember the smell of the limo, how Rachel looked as she sat in her car seat, the sound of the tires as we drove through the cemetery, even the smell in the air when we got out. All of these things come rushing back as I write these words. The tidal wave has never really *stopped*; it has just eased up over the years, not as large, but it is still as heavy as it was that day.

While that day may have been hard to stop my thoughts from raging on, looking at my daughter's sad face put things into perspective for me. I wasn't the only one hurting, and I had to keep myself held together so that she knew I would be there for her too.

The pallbearers placed his tiny little casket, only three feet long, on the platform over the grave. The graveside ceremony began, also led by Deb, after everyone was seated or standing where they were able to find a spot under the tent that had been erected around the grave site. I don't remember all that was said because all I could do was focus on that tiny little casket. This poem, an old Native American poem

from what I was told, was read by one of our friends at the
end of the graveside ceremony:

> *Do not stand at my grave and weep;*
> *I am not there. I do not sleep.*
> *I am a thousand winds that blow.*
> *I am the diamond glints on snow.*
> *I am the sunlight on ripened grain,*
> *I am the gentle autumn rain.*
> *When you awaken in the morning's hush,*
> *I am the swift uplifting rush*
> *Of quiet birds in circled flight.*
> *I am the soft starts that shine at night.*
> *Do not stand at my grave and cry;*
> *I am not there, I did not die.*

I feel bad that I can't remember who read it. I know at
one point it was discussed that Dave would read it or possibly Heather. I was so focused on that tiny casket that I
honestly can't remember.

Once the graveside ceremony was over, family and
friends started to file out to return to their vehicles, and I
just stood beside the casket. As I stood there, touching that
box that now held my baby boy's body, I lost it. I did not
want to leave. I had been holding it together for so long at
this point, and the dam broke. I remember several people

surrounding me, holding me up as I leaned on that little casket where my youngest son's body lay.

This is where his body would be for all of eternity.

Never to grow up. Never to learn how to write his name. Never to learn how to tie his shoes. Never to learn how to count to ten. Never to annoy his siblings. Never to go to homecoming. Never to go to prom. Never to graduate from high school or college. Never to do anything past what his five months and six days of life afforded him.

I stood and cried for who knows how long, and I felt several people trying to help me move toward the limo. I leaned down and kissed the top of the casket. My last kiss to my baby boy.

As I walked away from the grave site, I had issues with leaving like that. My son did not come into this world alone or without anyone who loved him. I did not want the final moment of his body leaving this world to be one where he was alone without loved ones. Deb and I shared this feeling, but she also knew that this was most likely the last thing I needed to see. With the help of a few family members, she managed to get me back into the limo, and she stayed at the cemetery with the staff from the funeral home until everything was done.

The limo took us back to the funeral home, and from there we joined the family and friends at a small gathering. We were thankful for Dave and Opal getting the small local hall to get together at. I can't remember who got food, but we were definitely thankful to them as well. Opal seemed to be much calmer after the graveside service was over; she had more color back in her cheeks and seemed to be doing much better overall.

I truthfully don't have a lot of memories of the rest of that day, just a whirlwind of family members and friends giving hugs, sharing tears, someone forcing me to eat, and more tears. I really wish I could look back and say that I remember what happened or even who was there. There are some that I know were there, but past that, the memories are hazy of the rest of that day. I remember friends from high school and family members from both sides. Everyone was there, friends old and new. I have memories of a blur of faces and names, but I was so loaded with emotions that it is hard for me to pinpoint everything.

Everyone slowly dwindled out, and I know at some point that we finally went back to Mike and Heather's. I passed out on their couch after we got all the floral arrangements and memorial items situated from the gifts given to us at the funeral. I am not sure if it was from physical or mental exhaustion that I finally passed out; it could very well have been both.

There is one thought that I remember having at some point that evening: this is the start of the healing. This day, while it has been the culmination of the past week, is really the beginning, not the ending. How I handle things from this moment will dictate the rest of the days of my life. How I react to things from this moment will reflect on the memory of my baby boy. I know I slept, but dreams, for the first time since Zack's passing, eluded me. For that I was thankful.

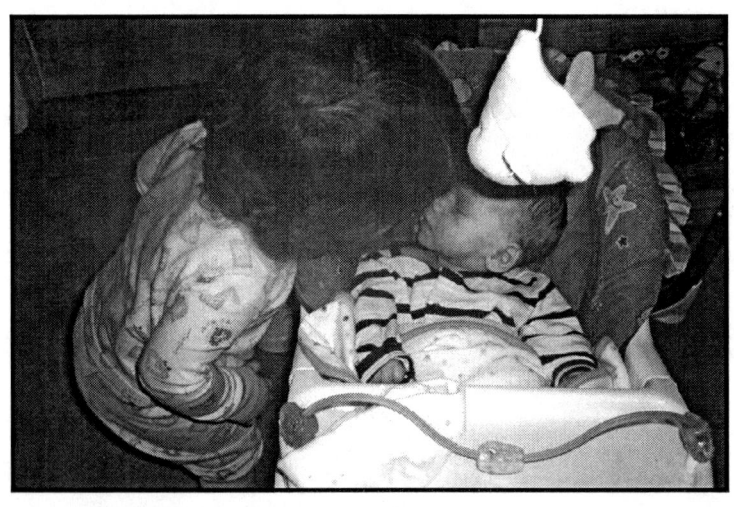

Rachel and Zackary. She had to check on him in his swing
because he made a little noise. Ever the protective big sister.

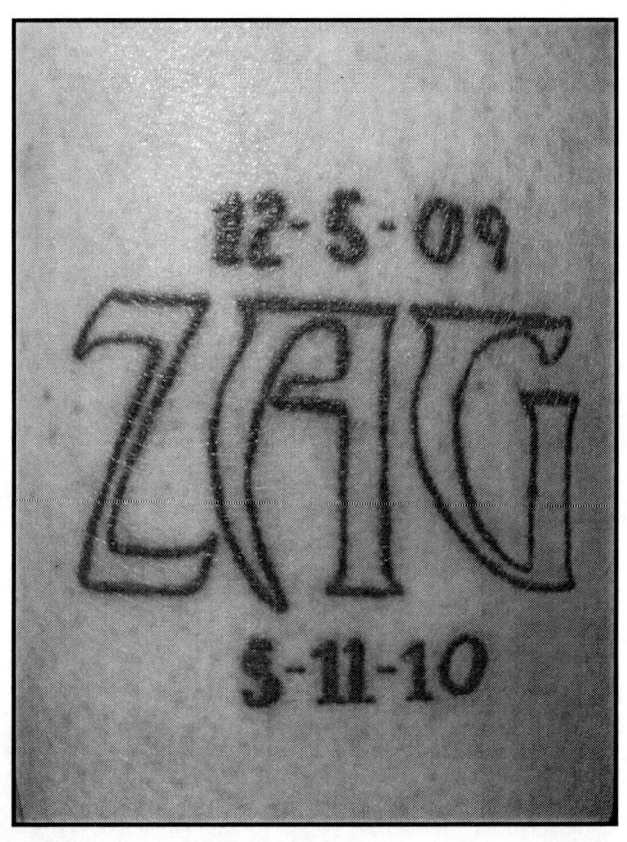

My tattoo in memory of Mr. Man. The pain was worth it because it gave me something to focus on. This is the outward expression of the hole in my heart that I have since losing Mr. Man's light from this world.

10

THE FIRST DAY OF HEALING

The day after the funeral was really the first day of coping with everything from the past week. The whole time from Zack's passing through to the funeral was merely getting by. I knew that I would not be able to start coping with this tragedy until the chaos of family and the funeral was done. I have always been the rock in my family, and I knew that if I would have let myself completely go at any point prior to the funeral, I would not have been able to keep it together.

Don't get me wrong, I mourned, I cried, I got angry, and I definitely had moments of uncontrolled emotion. However, I never let it *fully* out because I was not sure I would be able to reign it back in when I needed to.

At some point during that day after the funeral, we went back to our "home." The place we shared with Zack. The place that held all of our belongings was no longer feeling like a *home*. This was the place where my youngest child took *his last breath* at five months and six days old. It was hard to walk back into this place and realize that what used to be five people living there would never again be five, but four.

We went about trying to get things back in order. At some point during the previous week, my husband and Devin had taken down Mr. Man's bassinet and playpen and had managed to get most of his belongings out of the immediate view of all of us. These items were still in the house, just not right where they could be seen.

There was laundry that needed to be done, a kitchen and a bathroom to clean, sweeping and vacuuming to get done, and a myriad of other normal household chores. We tackled things one room at a time, working as a team while keeping Rachel occupied. We still spent time at Mike and Heather's because we did not think we could handle being home all the time for a while.

At some point that night, these were the words I wrote:

> *So here we are. Me rambling, you reading—and both of us know we are crazy.*
>
> *Today is day one of really starting to heal, and it has been touch and go. I have had some good moments, some bad moments, some pissed-at-the-world moments, and, well, you get the picture.*

Right now it is one of those in-between moments. I've got a migraine—meds are not working the greatest, watching my oldest and two of my nieces be annoying as hell to each other while Rachel annoys the piss out of everyone because she can, and I think...I think I can do this.

Then there was about an hour ago, trying to fold a load of laundry (because after a week of not being at the trailer, the cleaning fairs STILL did not show up), and there it was—some of Mr. Man's clothes. A sleeper, a onesie, and his bathrobe—things he wore a lot—and out of habit, I folded them and set them aside, just like I do with everything else. Then when I started telling Devin to put away certain things, I realized what I had done—and I felt kinda stupid that I did not catch it before then. It reminded me of after Mom died. A few months after Mom passed, I was trying to make something (for the life of me, I can't remember what), and I could not remember what it was that Mom used to do special with this recipe. And so I decided to call her, dialed the number, listening to it ring, then the message came that the phone number was no longer in service. And for a brief moment, I actually thought something was wrong—then it hit me like a ton of bricks that I was being stupid and forgetful of everything that had happened.

Back to now. Everyone still asking me how I am doing, am I okay, do I need anything. And I know that everyone means well, but at the same time, I just want to scream if one more person asks me that. At the same time though, I know that most people do not know what to say in this situation regardless if they have been through it or not, so it is all they know to do—just make sure we are okay.

I sit here and think about the whole grieving process. I think about all the emotions that they say you will go through, and then I think about the fact that the whole grieving process thing is just so that people have something to say.

In any event, I'm not really sure about what to really say to everyone—you know, all the people that don't know what to say to me.

I hurt, I cry, I get pissed, but that is all because I can't find a reason for all of this. I still have peace. I have peace in knowing my Mr. Man only knew love, purity, family, laughter, joy, and no pain. I have peace in knowing he is with one of his grandmothers, a grandfather, and many others.

Anyway, for those of you out there that don't know what to say to me, take comfort in knowing I feel the same. But we will get through this—I have faith.

I am off to scream at a migraine.

Much love to you all.

I was at a point where the logical side of me knew I had to move on with life, and there was my heart that was broken. Forever. Nonrepairable. My heart wanted the world to stop spinning and for everyone still breathing to acknowledge my pain. I wanted everyone to acknowledge my son, my baby boy.

Then the logical side reared its ugly little head again and said, "No, not everyone can handle this. You are strong, and *you* are a survivor." Stupid little voice. That part of me did *not* know what it was talking about. I was not a survivor. I was a sufferer. I was broken, and no doctor would be able to fix me. I wanted everyone to leave me alone. I wanted everyone to stop asking me if I was doing okay. I would never be "okay" again.

I felt at this point that I knew I would live my life, but I had no idea if I would *honestly* survive and come out on the other side. I was hurting on a whole new level that I had never really known before. I had overcome so much at this point in my life, and I really felt like the universe had it out for me. It seemed that every time I had things going my way, I was knocked flat on my back each. I began to wonder how many times I was going to be able to be knocked out flat before I wasn't able to get back up again.

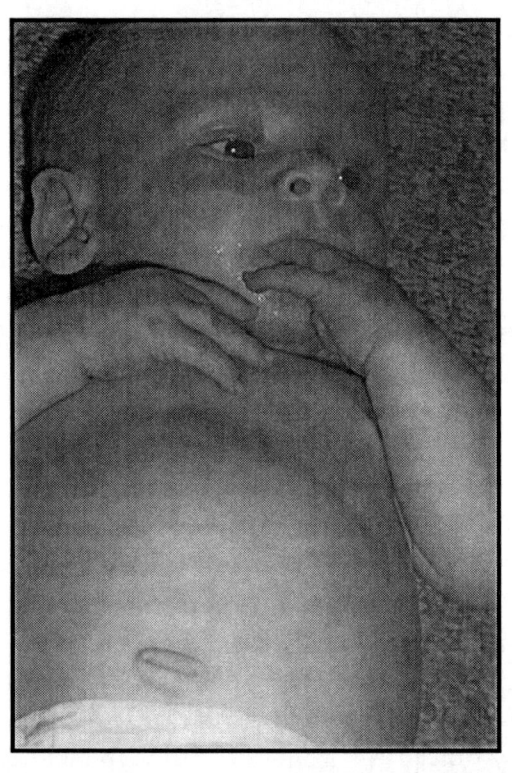

Mr. Man loved chewing on his fingers and was even happier if he could be without clothing. Who was I to object?

Mr. Man and Devin. Goodness gracious,
was it hard to keep clothes on that little boy.

11

READY OR NOT

Now, I can honestly say that I was not ready to start coping with this. Even though I knew I had to, for the sake of my children still with me if for no other reason. I just did not know how to process everything. I knew my beliefs, and I knew that I was not alone on my journey. I knew that I was not alone in my mourning, yet I did not know how to take that *first* step toward healing as it was a tough step.

A few days after the funeral, I did another journal entry:

Well, tonight was one more night in my healing—not sure exactly what that healing yet entails, but I am sure I will know when I get there. Last night I had a migraine, ended up back in the ER to get rid of it, and I'm not sure if it is just because everything is so fresh or if it is the effects of the medication, but every time I woke up, I caught myself looking for Zack, and then being crushed all over again because the realization came back hard that he is not here in the flesh anymore.

Okay, seriously—why me? Why my family? SOMEONE needs to find that answer. If I can be given an answer for that one, I might be able to tolerate the pain and hurt and eventually deal with it.

It still all seems like a nightmare that I should wake up from. I see everything and everyone around me going about their daily lives—including myself because I have—and I can't help but think that this just is not right! Why is this going on? How can this continue to be our "norm" when it is no longer the same?

We hold each other, we cry together, we share the pain, the hurt, we share it all, but I can't help but feel angry that THIS is something that we have to share. I shared everything with my family up to this point— just as they shared with me—so why is this something given to us to share as well?

I know, anger is just one more step in the whole grieving process—you're not telling me anything I do not already know. But the thing is, I have every right to be downright PISSED OFF!!!! And the diagnosis of SIDS (or now they call it SUIDS—Sudden Unexplained Infant Death Syndrome) that tells us *nothing, that gives us nothing to go on. As messed up as it sounds, I would have rather them tell me some major genetic disorder, at least then I would have found comfort in the fact that he would not have suffered, and this was a way of his body avoiding more severe pain. Not that I wouldn't have been pissed then too—but at least it would have been SOMETHING!*

And then I am sitting here, angry at myself because I got my tubes tied. I can't even try having another child because of that. Now before any of you blow a gasket, I know I can't replace him, I can't fill the void, and another child would not make me heal any quicker, but dammit, I wanted to RAISE three children. But because I was so gung ho on getting my tubes tied, now I feel like I let everyone down by getting it done.

Today is the birthday of my spirit sister Earth, and today is also her rebirth in her spiritual walk—very symbolic in that aspect. I can't help but wonder where I stand spiritually and how to explain it. I looked to my faith to give me peace, and I got it. Never ask for what you're not ready to receive, and I needed the peace to be able to cope, and I was granted it. But there is a difference between peace and happiness. I am not sure if I will ever be 100% happy again after this, but I will certainly be the best I can be for my other two children. But as for spiritually, I have not faltered from my faith,

and I am not questioning my faith. I am just question-
ing where I stand, what I should do, and how I should
do it. I am questioning what path is really the best for
me now, if it even changed at all.

And then there is my oldest—he is a whole new ball
of wax. Ever since that fateful night, he has been look-
ing for signs from his brother that he is okay, that he
still loves him, etc. We won't go into details, but let's
just say I now have a whole new issue with baby dolls.
Before now, he was always intrigued by the paranor-
mal, and now, I think it is even more so. He seems to be
obsessed with the thought of his brother sending him a
message over and over again. How do I help HIM deal
with all of this when I myself am having troubles???

So where do I go from here? I know that I have no
other choice but to keep moving on—but am I insane
for hoping against hope that I get a miracle to have
another child? Am I insane for blaming myself and
feeling like shit because I got my tubes tied against what
my family really wanted? Am I just insane all around?
I am so hurt, confused, upset, angry, pissed at myself for
being selfish.

Maybe it will all eventually come to me, but then
again, who knows.

Thank you for reading my ramblings—I hope they
make more sense to you than they do to me. Who knows,

*maybe if you understand them, you can explain a thing
or two to me so I will understand something amidst all
this chaos.*

I was at a point of needing to deal with my own grief, and then as a mom I had to help my other children through their grief. Rachel was the hardest in terms of understanding because at the time, she was only two years old. She knew that her baby brother Zack wasn't there with us anymore, but she did not understand the whys or where he could possibly be. Devin, on the other hand, had a perfect understanding. He unfortunately had already dealt with grief and loss already at his young age. He was almost five years old when my mom passed away, and that, unfortunately, initiated him into the world of what it is like to lose someone you love.

Helping Devin with things was difficult; he wanted a sign that Mr. Man was okay, and I couldn't give that to him. I could tell him that while he wasn't with us physically, he would always be with us in our hearts. I could tell Devin that I believed that Mr. Man was with our loved ones that have passed on before. I could not tell him that I knew this for certain, nor could I give him a sign about that.

I didn't know how to help him understand these things. I know that faith is something you believe in but can't see, and that it is there to help you through both the good and the bad times in your life. I never have pushed faith or religion on my children, and this was one of those times that I had to let him roam through his own mind. Regardless of what your faith is in, you can't reach out and touch your faith. You can't take a picture of it, but you still know what it means to you. I was faced with the challenge of helping him cope and also helping him find his own path of faith.

I was at a standstill with what to do. I was so angry about what had happened to my family, our friends, and most of all, Mr. Man. I knew I probably should have grounded myself, done meditation, prayed, or done something to refocus my energies; however, I was not sure I was ready to. At least by feeling angry, I was feeling *something*. I was afraid of becoming numb. I needed to continue to feel, whatever those emotions may be. I needed to have them so I knew I was still living. I knew that if I gave in to the numbness, I might not ever come back. I didn't want to live like that…a shell of my former self. That is not what I wanted to do in memory of my son. I did not want to do that to my other two children; they deserved so much better than that.

The remainder of that week was mostly a series of going through the motions to get through each day. Each day became a little easier to get up and start my day, even though I still woke up with the first thought of checking on the kids…all three of them. I would check on Rachel first because she was the closest. I would then go to Devin's room and check on him. Then I would sit in the living room, in the quiet of the morning, and "talk" to Zack.

Yes, I do know that makes me sound crazy, but I just knew that he could hear me. I could feel his spirit, and it gave me comfort. Even if that comfort was only for a few minutes each morning. Each day became a little easier to maneuver through, even though I still broke down and cried my eyes out at least once a day.

At some point during that first weekend, my thought and feelings started to make sense with each other. I'm not sure if I had reached a breaking point or if things just started to click into place, but regardless, things started to make sense. I had been having issues with insomnia since Zack passed away, and almost two weeks after he left us, in the wee morning hours, these are the words I wrote:

> *Well, I have reached an epiphany, and while to me it makes sense, I'm sure that others will think I am completely off my rocker, while others will simply think it's time for me to seek medication.*
>
> *Zack was given to me for a reason, and his death and the ensuing heartbreak that I feel was also for a reason, and I think I have made sense of it in my own twisted mind.*
>
> *Everything in life is two-sided—thus the meaning of the yin and the yang. Zack brought me great joy, a*

joy that I shared freely with those that I love. And with that joy now comes just as deep of a pain. That is also shared with those that I love, but with a heavy heart because that was not my intention for them to experience the pain. But I have realized that my family out there in my little "clan," as I call it, chose me and my family to share their joys, sorrows, and pains with them. They too realize that they will share those same things with me.

Now for the understanding.

Zackary—my little Mr. Man, my precious happy adorable little boy—was destined to give us so much joy because he knew the pain would be great when he left. And I believe that the reason that child was such a happy baby and always smiling is because he knew in some way of infinite wisdom that we will never understand—that his time here with us was going to be short, and thus he was going to enjoy every minute of it and make us all as happy as he could while he was here so that we would have nothing but wonderful memories of him to cherish, remember, share, and keep with us always.

I also believe that Mr. Man's purpose was even greater than that—that his purpose was to help me grow, help me be stronger than I ever thought I could, help me see a part of me that I never knew honestly existed. Even though as I sit here and put these thoughts into words, I'm shedding tears of sorrow for losing him, I believe I understand more than I ever thought I would.

And his purpose was not only for me, even though as his Mommy I tend to be partial, but it was for all of us—to teach us that we are not only strong as individuals, but that together there is nothing we can't get through. As a family he taught us that we can never hug our kids enough, say "I Love You" enough, or take enough pictures, but in the end, the bonds are never broken, the memories will always be there, and that person that we loved sooo damn much will always be in our hearts, not to mention be there with us as a part of our very soul.

Mr. Man has also done something spectacular for me—he has helped me realize that I am not just a mom, wife, sister, but that I am someone important to those that I love more than I can ever put words to. Now I am not saying that I never felt important because I have felt important to the ones that I love; what I mean by this is that I finally understand the importance of where this cog fits into this machine of my family. Without each cog, this machine does not run right, and I have finally come to understand the importance of where I fit in to all this craziness that is my family that I love so dearly.

Mr. Man also did something for this family unit as a whole—he brought us closer, showed us how much each of us means to each other, and made all of us realize that without the others, we're lost, which is how we feel without him. However, he also showed us that together, as a whole, we can make it through anything. Maybe one battle will only bruise us, and other battles—such as losing Zackary—will scar us for life. But regardless of the outcome, we will still be together.

I also realized that my family are the rocks that keep me grounded, and Zack is that little invisible push or kick in the ass when I need it.

So I guess I need to thank you all for being there, being who you are to me, and loving me the way you do while letting me love you in my own way. I need to thank you all for loving Zack the way you have and missing him and cherishing his memory.

My children—Devin, Rachel, and Zackary—I love you for all that you have given me, all that you will give me, and for all that you are.

And my family—Kara, Earth, Heather, Opal, Dave, Ryan, Mike, Deb, Shawn, and all the other crazies that I adore and can't type all in one list—thank you for not only loving me and my children, but for letting us love you. Thank you for sharing my joy and my pain, even though at times it may feel unbearable.

I feel like a weight has been lifted from my shoulders after writing this. I don't know if it's because I have created my own reasoning and it makes sense to me, or if it's simply a part of the grieving and healing process, or both. But I will say this: Zack was a joy, a gift, and a beautiful example of pure love, and for that I am thankful for the five months I was given. I will cherish those memories, those moments, and as I continue to heal through writing, crying, and being a blubbering idiot, I hope that all of you who share this grief with us will also heal with us. One moment at a time, and someday when our time comes, each of us will be welcomed into the afterlife, whatever it is you believe, by the open arms of one little boy that loved us so much and knew that we loved him in return.

Enough of my rambling.

Thank you, and I love you, my wonderful, yet crazy, family.

I look back on those words, and I meant every single one of them. Every child is a gift, and Zack was a true gift to me and my family in more ways than one. He brought to us a joy unlike any we have ever known. He gave something special to everyone who was touched by his life. That something special is only known by each individual, but it was shared with a loving heart by a little boy who knew nothing *but* love. His passing brought us pain and heartbreak like most of us had never known, but that is the balance of life. Without the good, the bad would be too hard to survive. Without the bad, we wouldn't know how to appreciate the good.

I knew at this point that I was going to make it, one way or another. I just had to figure out the how. I knew that I was still strong in my beliefs. I believe that nothing happens as a mere coincidence, but how I react to each of the events in my life is the true testament to my character. Each day was a new beginning with its own trials, tribulations, frustrations, and emotions. I knew that with each reaction I had to these things, I was showing not only what I was made of, but I was also showing Devin and Rachel that their mother is a survivor. By showing them this, which is a hard lesson for me to live through, it showed them that they too can be survivors. It also showed them that we can do this together, as a family, and that we may be broken, bruised, and bloody, but we are *not* beaten. Those thoughts were a driving force for me mentally to keep going every day.

No, Zack was no longer physically with me, but he was there in every breath, every beat of my heart, and every thought. He still is to this very day, and he will continue to be until the day I die. I now needed to figure out *how* to live my life in a way that would not only show Devin and Rachel how to survive, but also show myself that I'm made of tough stuff, and hopefully that Zack would be proud of his mommy. I knew that this had to be done, but figuring out the how was the hardest part. How do you take a pile of ashes and turn it into a phoenix?

I felt like that was what I needed to do. I had to gather the ashes that my life had turned into and find the mold to turn them and turn myself into the phoenix and rise above it all.

Emotional baggage is a very heavy thing, and when holding on to it all, I knew there was no way that I was going to soar above the clouds and prove to myself and my children that we can do this. I had to sort through each piece, weed out the bad, and cultivate the seeds for the good. That was a lot easier said than done. I knew it *needed* to be done, but doing it was going to prove to be the hard part.

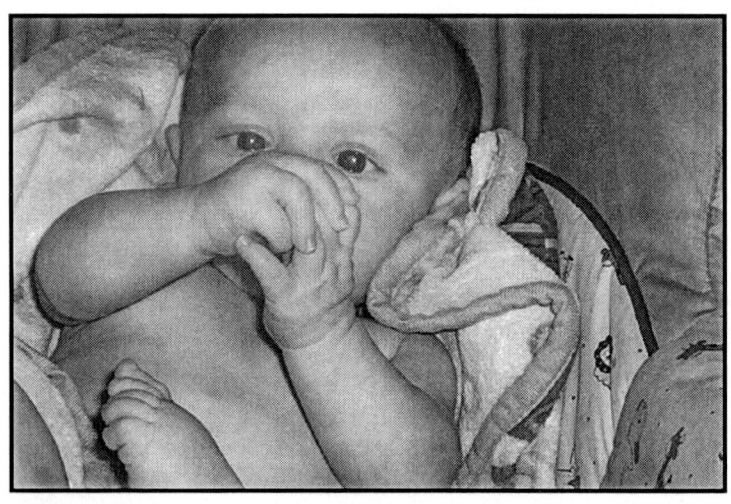

Zack was so fun to watch, especially when he would focus on his hands and feet, how they moved, and even more comical when he realized it would hurt if he bit them!

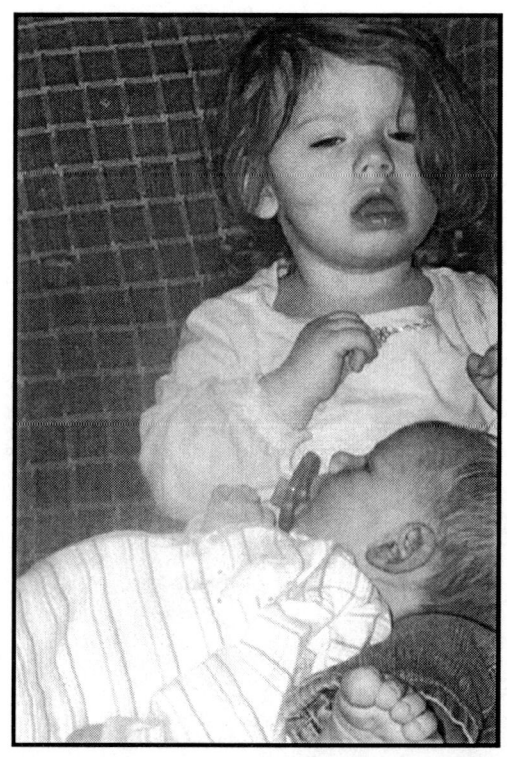

Rachel and Mr. Man. She was getting mad because
we told her to leave his pacifier alone!

12

THE MONTHS AFTER

The day after my breakthrough of sorts was the seventh anniversary of my mother's passing. In many ways, I like to think that she guided me from the other side to help me find the first steps of my journey. My mother was always there for me for as long as I can remember, and it only made sense to me that she found a way to continue to do it after she was no longer among the living. May is truly the hardest month of the year for me to get through. Zack passed on the eleventh, my mom on the twenty-fifth, and then try to celebrate my birthday on the twenty-sixth? That hasn't happened in as many years as my mom has been gone. Mother's Day is now a hard day for me as well. Things are just not the same.

The next few weeks pass in a bit of a blur. After my birthday, Devin's birthday was in early June, my husband's birthday, then Father's Day. We did our best to keep on an even keel, but allowed ourselves to express our emotions when we needed to. I would find myself watching television, and I would start crying after seeing a diaper commercial. This was perfectly normal, I was told, but it was still very hard to deal with. I don't like being normal because I'm just *not*. I am crazy, weird, unusual, and anything but normal. When I was told that everything I was doing and going through was a normal step in the grieving process, I had to wonder what type of grief they were talking about.

I learned at a very young age that there are different types and levels of grief. I have grieved the passing of grandparents, aunts, uncles, friends, and all ages of people. I had even been on the other side of losing a child, as I had friends that have been on this journey longer than I, and I knew from the outside how difficult it could be. The grief I have from losing my mother was the worst I had ever dealt with up to this point, and that didn't come anywhere close to how I felt after losing Zack. I still wonder to this very day, how can the grieving process be defined as "normal" when for each person and each death, it is a different experience? Is that the "normal" part of it?

Friends and family continued to check in on us, but I could tell that it was hard for them to do. I knew that every single one of them was hurting, but they felt that they needed to make sure that we were okay. This began to strain some relationships. We didn't really do much outside of the four of us and our house. It was difficult to just go do things when I knew I was not at a point emotionally that I could handle everything. I knew that over time, things would get better. At that point though, time was moving too slowly for me.

Some friends over the following months began to wane, while others stepped in even closer. Of those that fell back, I don't blame them; I completely understand why they chose to step back. Some of them stepped back because they did not know what to say or how to handle things with us; others just did not know how to face the reality of someone they knew losing a child. I wish that things had been different, that I would have known what to say to each of them to help ease their discomfort, but life has a way of getting you to where you *need* to be, not always where you *want* to be.

Each day was another milestone. During this time, we sorted out how to work with each other, and we also enrolled Devin in homeschooling because it was a better fit. We did not think that some individuals that were in authoritative positions at his school handled the aftermath of dealing with Zack's passing very well. We felt it was better to handle things our way. Grief is a personal process, and they were trying to push the issue with Devin, and I was not going to allow anyone to pressure any of us into processing those emotions until the time was right.

This is another case of not blaming anyone, but it is definitely a situation that should have been handled differently than it was. At the time of Mr. Man's passing, Devin was a month away from turning twelve. That is a very sensitive age, and to try to force the issue of coping with such a tragedy was not the best choice of things that the school could have or should have done.

My husband had started, and later quit, truck driving school, and I was unemployed but managed to get little temporary jobs here and there. Things were tight, but we were surviving. I was still battling insomnia, but it was getting better.

Sometime in the middle of that summer, I had been watching early morning television and stumbled upon a show for crochet and knitting. I had known how to crochet since I was in my early teens, but I was not very good at it. This show made the proverbial light go off in my head. I had all my mom's crochet supplies, along with some yarn, lying around the house, and I decided to see if I could follow along with some of the tips and techniques they were demonstrating. Enter from stage left my new form of therapy: crochet.

For the months following Zack's death, sleep eluded me more than a few hours at a time. So during my waking hours, I did what I knew: I searched for a job, took care of my kids, read any book I could get a hold of, and I crocheted. When you are only sleeping about three to four hours at a time with twenty to twenty-four hours in between, you tend to get a lot of things done. At one point I had two large boxes of yarn and about thirty books sitting on my entertainment center. Both of those stacks would dwindle faster than I really care to admit.

I was reading anything and everything to keep my brain occupied enough that it was not running at top speed about the woulda, coulda, shouldas; and then the crochet kept both my brain and my hands busy. The librarians knew me by name because I was in there so frequently. For quite some time I could rattle off my library card number because of entering it so many times on their website when I would log in to reserve books. I have always had a love of books, but I let it explode during this time simply to keep myself occupied.

At the same time, my crochet project was beginning to take shape. I had started working what is commonly referred to as the granny square stitch. I just kept working and working it. At one point, I was asked what I was making, and without much thought, I decided it would be an afghan for my bed.

The granny square I was working on got to be about three feet square, and I decided to take a different approach with how I wanted the afghan to look. I finished off the round I was on and started making smaller ones. When all was said and done, there were seventy-two squares and two strands of yarn used throughout the entire afghan. This was a huge, warm, heavy behemoth, and I made it. That was the true start of my crochet passion, and I still have that passion to this very day.

Crochet has become a therapy of sorts over the years since losing Mr. Man. I can look back on a project, and I can see the stitches that I worked when I was not upset, and then I can see a total difference in the stitches I worked when I *was* upset. Even though there were obvious differences, it was amazing to see the finished product; knowing that I literally put my heart and soul into that project for someone was wonderful. To know that I was able to create something beautiful out of all my pain, that would make me feel like I accomplished some small feat.

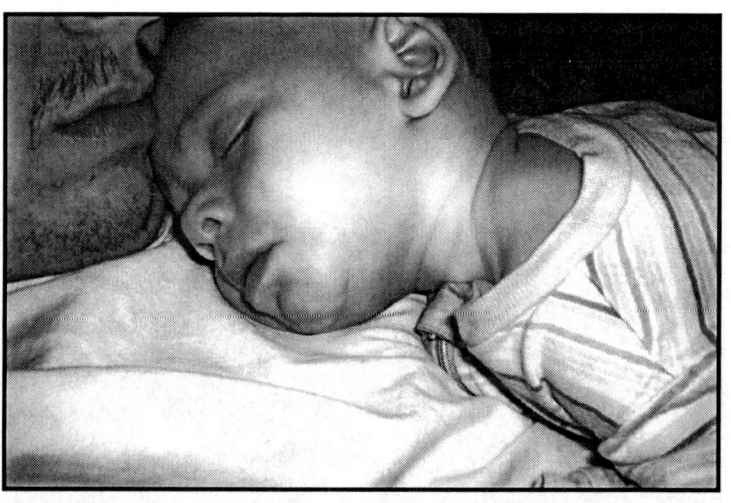

Mr. Man. We call this the "turtle" picture. His little green sleeper with him stretching his neck out like that just made all of us think of a little turtle.

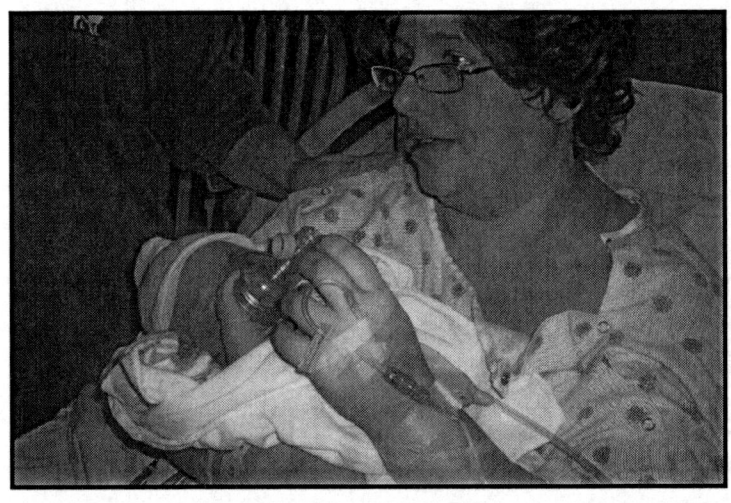

Mommy and Zackary. I was just so happy. I couldn't help but cry absolute tears of joy that this boy was finally in my arms.

13

LOOKING AT THE PROOF

At some point during that summer, we finally got the copy of the autopsy report. I know, I know, everyone asked us why we would want to see that, but I had to know. I needed to see for myself what they said. I needed to know that they checked everything and still did not come up with an answer. I kept hoping that there was some miniscule "thing" that was wrong. I kept hoping that there was something to tell us that this was for the best, that there was a defect in something…anything. But there was nothing. The autopsy report said just what the local coroner had told us: nothing was found.

I did some research on SIDS, on possible causes, looking for anything that might explain things. The only thing I have ever found is that there is a hypothesis about the possibility of a "delay in the serotonin-binding nerve pathways in the brain." For some reason, this hypothesis seems to think that the delay of these nerve pathways causes there to be issues with the infants' abilities to awaken when there are problems. Until this can be proven, disproved, or even tested for, SIDS will continue to be something that leaves parents wondering, second-guessing, and in a permanent state of "what if." Someday I can hope that it will merely be a thing of the past and that Angel Parents will no longer have to deal with the taboo issues of discussing their lost little angels.

I know that there are many different things discussed online, in person, in doctor's offices, health departments, etc., of what the actual cause of SIDS is. But the harsh reality is that there is a reason that it is unexplained, sudden, and never has answers. One major reason is that with an infant or child death, yes, the autopsy is a legal requirement in most cases, but without knowing a direction to look into, the officials are only going to look at the standard things to look at. This includes the body, blood, and brain. If those standard things don't indicate anything is wrong or amiss, the determination is SIDS/SUIDS.

There are several hypotheses and ideas about the causes, but as of yet, there are no definitive testing methods to help prove or disprove any of them. This needs to change, but until it does, this will continue to happen, this will continue to leave Angel Parents wondering, and this will continue to break hearts and shatter souls. That is why communication is so important. That is also why I felt it so important to write this, to bring this to the average person, to tell the story of Mr. Man and his life. If by going through the pain of reliving this journey to write this book will make a difference for one parent, one family, the memory of one child…then all of this was worth it.

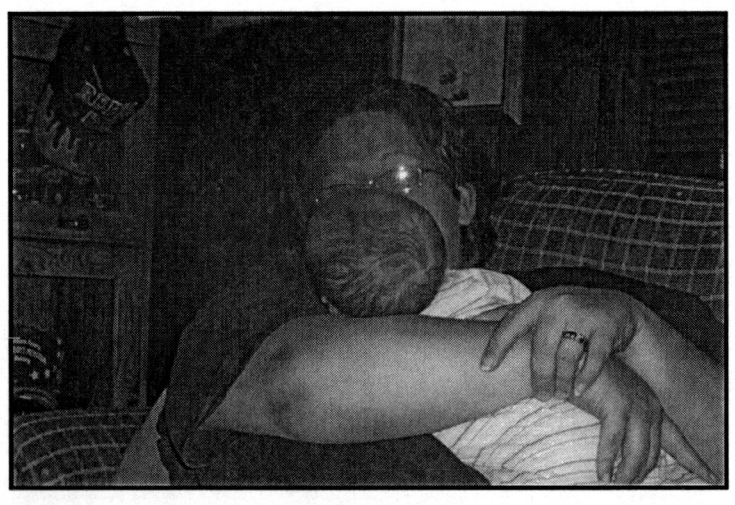

Mommy and Zack. One of my favorite things to do then, and still is, is to cuddle and smooch on my kids. It was just much easier when they were this little!

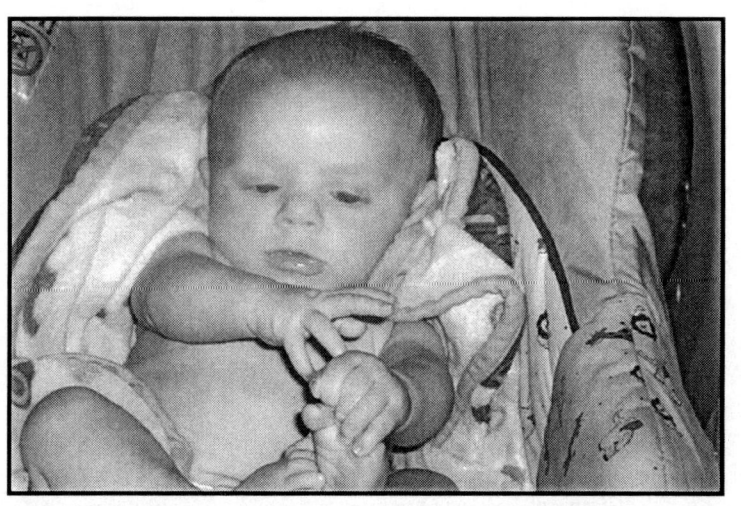

Mr. Man—he was so entertained by his toes!

14

Autumn Arrives

Through everything, I kept thinking about why my family was "chosen" to deal with this tragedy. I kept wondering how we were going to make it through the holidays, his birthday, our birthdays, and every other special day that came along.

Devin's school year started, and we were able to keep busy with that, and of course, Rachel always kept us occupied. Things were still a roller coaster, but we were making it. We still weren't very active with friends and family, but I just was not ready for that yet.

In many cultures and beliefs, the time of Halloween is a time of reverence for those who have passed away, a celebration of ancestors and a celebration of the lives of those who recently passed. That first Halloween, it really hit home for me *why* so many cultures and beliefs believe that. We went to the cemetery, and as I sat there between the two graves, I thought about all that the past year had brought to my family and I.

The whole point of giving reverence to those who have passed before us is simple: reverence to our ancestors as none of us would be here if not for them. Take that thought process and then realize that I was sitting there on the grass between two graves, one being that of my mother (my ancestor), and the other grave being that of my son (my future). Nothing in my life could have ever prepared me for this situation, nor did I feel that anything I had done in life had been so terrible to warrant this type of karmic repercussion.

Once again, that lightbulb went off above my head. I had never had an easy life. I was the youngest child, raised by a single mother who always struggled to provide for her family. I had one marriage that did not last, yet was able to move on and get married again. I took care of my mother in her final days through her fight with cancer, and now I was dealing with the death of my youngest child. Each thing I had survived in my past prepared me for the next event in my life. Had I not had the childhood I had, I may not have been able to handle everything that led up to my first marriage ending. If I would not have had my first marriage end the way it did, I may not have known what I wanted differently out of a relationship before my second marriage. Had I not lost my mother the day before my twenty-fourth birthday, I may not have had the "intestinal fortitude" to handle the death of my youngest child.

Each event built upon the other. Each event taught me something I would need for the next phase of my life. Now, the trick was to figure out what this particular event in my life needed to teach me. I have heard the saying that "what doesn't kill you makes you stronger." My response to that is that by now, I should be strong enough to bench-press a tank!

I decided that my son's death was not going to be without meaning. I decided that his short five months on this earth were not going to be forgotten. I did not believe in coincidences. I was given each of the events in my life to learn something, and I was going to sort through it and come out on top. I knew that with the foundation I had in myself and in my faith that I could make it through this; I just had to take the right steps. I knew that there would be times I would fall, but I also knew that I would get right back up and carry on.

How I approached this from here on out would entirely be up to me, yet I knew the groundwork was already laid out in front of me. It was up to me to decipher how to make it all work, how to put it all together, and how to solve this puzzle. My life had never been easy, so I don't know why

I deluded myself into thinking that dealing with this, the darkest hour of my life, would be easy at all.

When we left the cemetery, I had a new outlook on everything, a new understanding of my purpose, and a new goal to achieve. My outlook was that this was not done to punish me or teach me some lesson, but to help me be the person I need to be. Zack was brought into my life to show me the meaning of pure, unadulterated joy. His death was showing me that I am strong. I am a survivor. I am capable of doing anything that I set my mind to.

My understanding of this situation and my feelings is that I no longer had to worry about everyone else. I had always been the one to make sure that things were taken care of, and I now needed to realize that I can't do that. I needed to be me. I needed to be there for my family how I was able to, but not stretch myself so thin that I was burning the candle at both ends. I needed to allow others to take control of their situations and handle them on their own. I knew that I still wanted to be there to offer moral support, but I could no longer hold their hand throughout the entire situation. I realized that what I had been doing wasn't helping anyone—it was enabling them.

Goals are great to have and go hand in hand with one's purpose, and my new goal was to not only keep his memory alive, but also help others through their grief and sorrow. The death of a child through infant loss or miscarriage is still a very taboo subject, but I knew that I could help bring together those out there that suffered in silence every day. There are so many parents in the world that have suffered through the pain of a miscarriage but have been told, "You can try again" or "You didn't have the baby yet, you'll be fine." To me, the loss of a child at any age is still the loss of a child. No one else has the right to tell you that your baby wasn't as important as mine simply because they never had the chance to be born.

You can't compare the loss of one child to another simply because you see a physical difference from one to the other. Children are humans at any stage of development; they are not produce to pick and choose from. I knew that there were so many parents and family members that I could help in one way or another, and I was determined to make it happen.

Now, understanding, purpose, and goals are great, but implementation is the key. *That* is what had me stumped. Where do I begin? How do I start on this lofty set of goals I had created for myself? How do I keep it going once I do start? I knew the answers would come in time, but patience was, and still is, a virtue I have always had a problem with.

As we continued the drive home from the cemetery, I said a silent prayer: *Guide me down the right path. I owe this to my son, to myself, to Rachel, Devin, and to my mother. Give me the strength to see this through. Give me the patience to get through the rough patches. Give me the path to follow.*

After saying that, almost immediately, I felt an overwhelming sense of peace. I knew my prayer was heard and that the path and journey would not be easy, but I would not be doing it alone.

All of this from one visit to the cemetery, and while I knew my life would never be the same again, I *did* know that at some point, I would find my even keel again. I knew that by relying on the beliefs of my faith that I would make it through, one step at a time. The saying "The journey of a thousand miles begins with a single step" had never made any more sense as it did at that very moment in my life. I had already taken the first step. At this point I had taken dozens, but I now knew where I needed to walk. I felt that I had "mapped out" my path in a sense, and I was confident that I could achieve this, not only for myself and my family, but for Mr. Man's memory as well.

Mr. Man would love to sit for a bit in his car seat after we would get in the house. He would sit and babble on, and I miss that sound.

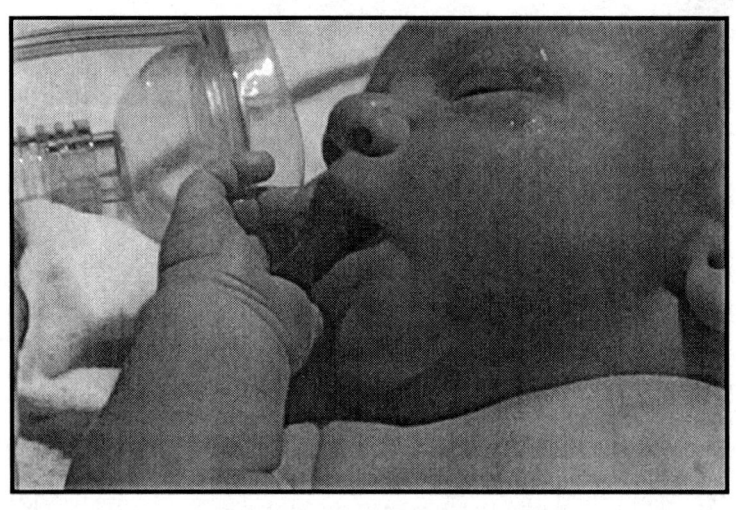

Mr. Man, the day he was born.

15

HOLIDAYS

Before I knew it, the holidays were upon us, and I still didn't have any answers as to how to get through them unscathed, but I had to try. I don't really remember too much of that first Thanksgiving without Zack. I know that probably sounds odd, but when I was trying so hard to just keep it together, everything else blurred into the background. I knew that spending time with friends and family is an important part of this holiday—it always had been—but this year was different. I was seeing things with a different view. I didn't think that Thanksgiving would have been as hard as it was, but then again we had never had the chance to celebrate all the good food and great company with Zack, so it was a rush of memories and thoughts that made things difficult. I knew that I would have speed bumps on my journey, and that the road ahead was not going to be an easy one. I had peace over some things, but not all. The first holidays without Zack made it very difficult to keep things in perspective. I consistently fought the anchor that threatened to pull me down every day.

We got through the dinner, and typically, the day after Thanksgiving meant putting up our tree and decorating the house. That year we weren't into decorating very much; between money being tight and our grief still overwhelming us, we weren't feeling very festive. We decided that we were going to get through Zack's birthday and make decisions then. This would have been his first birthday, December 5, 2010. This was a milestone for us; we made it to this point *mostly* intact, and we were still surviving.

On Mr. Man's first birthday, we got together with friends for dinner. It was really nice celebrating something with the family that *should* be celebrated. I know that Mr. Man was with us in his own way, but I wish he would have been there physically. I realize that is pretty much a *duh* statement, but it was such a milestone. He would have been *one* year old. To have the realization that he never got to see that milestone brought back a ton of memories again about all the things he would never do and the things that I would never see with him.

We continued to discuss decorations for about another week after Mr. Man's first birthday before we finally decided to get everything out and put up only what we felt needed to go up. That in itself was a trip down memory lane. Most of our decorations had some sort of sentimental value to them. Some of the decorations were my mother's, others were ones that Devin had made when he was younger, and some were just ones we purchased as a family. Each item that I pulled out of the box made me cry, and that is not an exaggeration. For me, there was a memory wrapped up in every single item, from the smallest ornament to the largest figurine.

I had a story for each item, and I proceeded to share with Devin and Rachel each story. Needless to say, decorating took much longer than it probably needed to, but I felt the need to share with them these bits of history. Decorating took almost two full days to complete, but at the end of the second day, I felt relieved. I shared those moments with my family and brought forth and shared memories that should never be forgotten.

That first Christmas celebration was difficult. That was the only big holiday we had celebrated with Mr. Man, so there were lots of memories, but not enough. He was only twenty days old at his first Christmas, so it wasn't like he would have known what was going on. He knew that he was surrounded by his family and that he was held and loved, but we don't have any of the great pictures of the faces he made from opening his own presents. He never got old enough to do that. We decided to not attend the big family Christmas gathering with my in-laws that year. I just could not face all of them, knowing that they were all going to be looking at me, at us, and thinking who knows what. I thought of every emotion and especially that they would feel bad for me and for my family. I just couldn't handle that so soon after losing Mr. Man.

We decided to celebrate our day with Triv and her family. She was really an amazing driving force for me to keep things together at that time. She let me cry when I needed to cry, scream when I needed to scream, and she always knew when I needed a hug.

When we arrived at her place, her kids helped us unload all the goodies from our van, and then she brought me a candle that was already lit. She told me that the candle would stay lit all day and that it was in memory of Zack. It was a physical representation of him since he couldn't be there himself. Needless to say, I cried like a baby.

We had our moments through the rest of the day that made us laugh, cry, and a few that made us scream. When you realize the fact that there were five children ranging in ages from thirteen years old down to two years old, it really was no surprise about the screaming. The two youngest, both girls, Rachel and Chandler, were only fifteen days apart. You could tell that they were close, like peanut butter and jelly, and they loved to drive the older kids crazy.

At one point, the two youngest were off watching some children's show, and the three oldest were playing cards. You would hear the little ones giggling, the older ones arguing about what card one of them played, and it just kept going. I remember just feeling totally at peace that entire day, almost as if I was recharging my batteries, so to speak. Triv's dad even came over and ate with us all, and all of the adults sat around and talked for what seemed like forever. It was a wonderful holiday that I will never forget.

When we left Triv's home late that night to go back to our house, I honestly felt that it was the turning over of a new leaf. I realized that it is okay for me to be angry. It is okay for me to cry when I need to. I also realized that it is okay for me to be strong. I'm not sure if Triv really knows the gift that she gave me that day or if she ever will fully know. No words could ever describe to her what that small act on one day in December meant. She gave me a respite from the outside world and let me focus on me and my family. She gave my children a happy memory amid a tough and emotionally draining year. She stood by my side and held my hand when others had faded into the background. No words I could ever say would truly ever tell her how much that meant. She will always hold a special place in my heart for that one day and also for so many others.

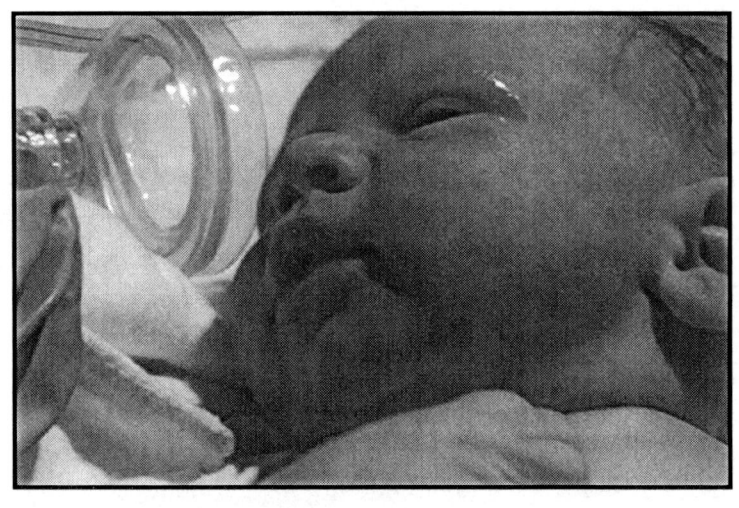

Mr. Man opening his eyes for the first time.

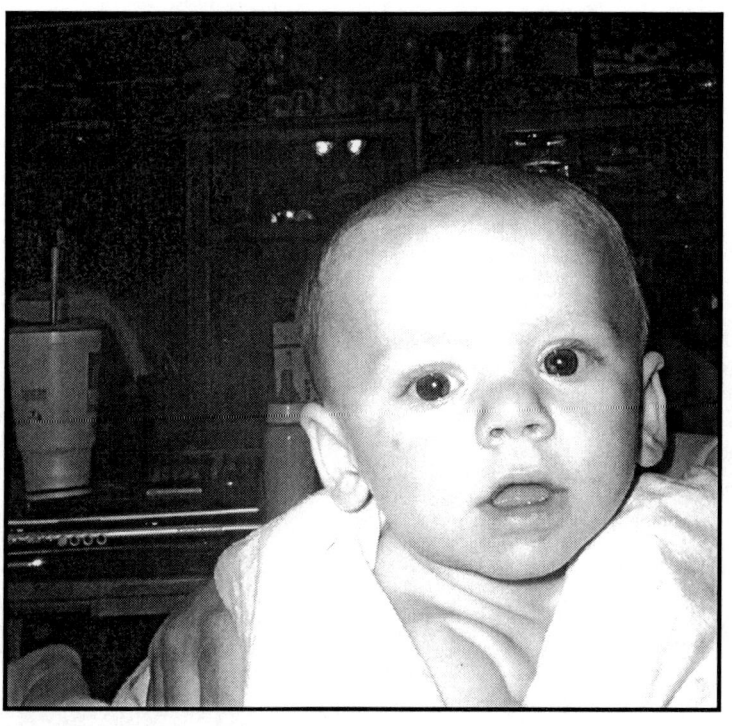

Mr. Man was always willing to look at the camera.
Such a beautiful boy.

16

STARTING A NEW YEAR

The rest of December went by remarkably uneventful, bringing in the New Year together as a family and realizing that 2011 was going to be full of firsts for all of us. I started blogging in early January, and while I was handling things as best as could be expected, I was dealing with a lot of issues. My first blog entry, while short, said so much:

1/6/2011

A new day—a new year—everything is new.
    But it isn't.
    I realized today, that blogging might be a great form of therapy. Time will tell if it really is or is not.

Let me explain a little bit.

I am the mother of three beautiful children. Devin, age twelve, Rachel, age two (almost three), and Zackary, forever staying five months and six days old. Now in reality, he would be thirteen months old as of yesterday, but we lost him to SIDS on May 11, 2010.

Since then, I have gone through every emotion possible; hurt, anger, fear, frustration, love, hate, and the list goes on. The only thing I never really experienced was denial. I went from hope to despair—I was hopeful they could save my baby, but when they told me they could not, I reached the depths of despair, totally skipping that whole denial phase.

Since then, it has been a focus of healing, learning, adjusting, and taking every day one minute at a time.

I have learned how to knit, how to do a million things with crochet, that my family and friends love my cooking even more than I thought they did, and that some people don't have what it takes to stand by you when your life is shattered. But I have been trekking on, and I will continue to do so until I am no longer breathing.

So here is my start—my new year—let's see where this goes—what I feel I have to blog about, and what I feel in general. Let's hope this is therapeutic, every little bit helps.

I blogged for several days in a row at first, trying to take advantage of the new form of "therapy" that I was trying. I had gotten to a point where I knew what I felt and I knew where I wanted to be, but the path between the two was hidden by a dense fog of war.

1/7/2011

Another day in the life of me. Once again going through the issues over getting my tubal. I know I know—who could have possibly known that we would experience what we did, so there was no way of knowing that getting my tubes tied would be a bad idea. I know this. I was also hell bent on getting them tied, I love being a mommy, but being pregnant isn't exactly my cup of tea. Pregnancy isn't kind to me, the hormones, the migraines, all the issues—the only awesome thing is knowing that this little creature is growing inside of me, and I'm creating life. That's it—everything else is painful, hard to manage, and downright miserable.

And now I want it for my family more than I ever have in the past, to make them happy.

I know I can't replace Zack; I would be stupid to even think so. Mr. Man was an incredible child, baby, and human being. He knew nothing but pure love, pure joy, and pure happiness, and he loved all of us in return with that pureness. To even think I could replace that; I would be out of my mind.

I just want my family to be happy, and a part of me wants another chance. Not to mention that it does not help right now that it seems like EVERYONE I know that is able to be is pregnant. Family, friends, and people I don't know but hear about.

Now I know, I should count my blessings, and I do. Devin, as much as there are days I would rather tie him to the ceiling fan, he is a joy in my life. We argue because we are too much alike. But I have done a damn good job with him. Granted, his father has nothing to do with him anymore, but I have given Devin a family and the foundation he needs to build on as he ages, and will one day leave my house without have to do on a day time talk show. He is smart, responsible, and capable—of course all of this when he wants to be, and I'm still very proud of him—even when I'm mad at him.

Rachel—that is another case of too much alike—she is my mini-me—110%. There are days I have thought of using Velcro to put her on the wall just long enough to be able to go pee by myself, but I still enjoy every minute I have with her, because one day, she will grow up, and it will be gone. She is smart—some days too smart for her own good—but she is also a joy.

But there is always going to be that missing link, and I am always going to feel a tad empty in that one spot in my heart, regardless if I would have no more children or a dozen more. I still am considering the opportunity to make my family happy and having another chance. I know that eventually I will either get lucky, or I will get old enough to realize that it will never happen, and I will deal with it, but until one or the other happens, I will just keep taking it one day at a time. That's all I can do.

To those that are pregnant—may your children be blessed, healthy, and everything they need to be, and that you want them to be, and more. May they always give you joy, drive you crazy, and worry you senseless when they grow up. And may you always have the ability to know when to cut the strings, and when to hold them tight. Above all else—always give them an extra hug and send it out to Mr. Man to share a little bit of that love with him.

Thanks for reading my rant—until the next post— enjoy your day.

That one was a bad day. I remember that one because it seemed like every time I turned around, someone else was pregnant. Here I was mourning and grieving over the loss of my child, and everyone else I knew was having them.

It seemed so unfair. It was hard to wrap my head around things. I was still having problems with my migraines; they would come and go at any point with no rhyme or reason, but I tried to work through them as much as possible. I was so open about things in my blog, as if I was writing to my best friend. I am not sure why I felt so free to be able to write the things I did, but that therapy idea might have helped. I felt like I was free to write and say whatever I wanted to. I know I didn't have to blog online, but at the same time, I felt that if I shared the things in my head in a way that my friends and family could read it, they might be able to understand me in a different way. Some did, some didn't, and I'm sure that some didn't read it. That is the nature of the beast. In the end, it helped me, and that is what seemed to matter.

1/9/2011

Okay—another day—and this—another headache. So I took my meds, I'm blogging—and hoping that maybe it will go away.

Had a messed up weekend with good points, low points, and scary points. Good points—had a WONDERFUL visit with a woman I call Super Shirley. I have been talking to her for about two years online and she has been a blessing in my life. Our relationship is how I wish most people were with others. We have vast differences in who we are—but we support each other in those differences—we respect those differences in each other—and I love her dearly for that acceptance that she has given me. It means more than she can understand.

The funny thing—I only met her in person for the first time, just a couple days ago—and I feel like I have known her all my life. She has been there with us through so much with losing Mr. Man because she herself has lost a child. She has listened to me rant, given me a shoulder, and encouraged me when I have needed it, and I believe I'm a better person for knowing her.

Another good point—I think my sister and I are back on the mend. This means so much to me. I have missed her, and I hope this is for good this time.

And yet another good point—we had company all weekend—our dear friend Seth came and stayed with us. He needed some time away, and we needed the distraction—it was a win-win situation.

Low points—the stupid vehicles want to be a pain; problems with both the van and the truck. Hopefully the van is better, but I am not sure how long it will stay that way—the battery decided to go stupid on us, and after being on the charger for forever—it started and has been working ever since. I am just hoping it keeps working. The truck needs a new battery, and a new radiator. Hopefully we will be able to start getting that taken care of.

Scary points—my sister had to go to the ER for her sugars being super high. I was glad she called me, but I was scared shitless until they said she could go home. After everything we went through when we were younger with our mom—I guess I scare easily with some stuff. But so far, she seems to be doing better, so let's keep hoping.

I made homemade Stromboli last night—turned out awesome—but way filling. Couldn't hardly eat a fourth of it, but go big or go home is my motto. If you are gonna make something—don't make it half-assed—and I certainly don't! For dessert I made chocolate heath cheesecake—and it was delicious.

Tomorrow starts another week—school—kids—clean house—etc. Hopefully I won't have the migraine at the end of the day.

As I have sat here and typed this—I realize that this blogging thing really is helpful to some extent so far. I feel that I can just throw it out there—and get things off my chest. I don't have to worry about whether or not someone has time to listen to me rant, or whether or not they even want to listen to me.

I can talk about anything from the mundane daily activities of my life, to the serious emotional issues I *have at the time, and you (whoever you are) can either decide to read it or not, and I don't feel like I'm imposing on anyone's time. I think that alone is a big help.*

And as for the more emotional issues—I keep having weird dreams. Dreams about Mr. Man and mom— dreams about things in the future that I have no idea what they are supposed to mean—dreams about the past that make my heart ache. It has been like this now for about three weeks. At least once a night, I wake up with a feeling like I should understand something from my dreams, but the only feeling I have when I wake up is confusion and hurt. This year my mom has been gone for eight years, and this year will be the one year mark of Mr. Man being gone. Two weeks apart I might add.

So I'm left wondering what I'm supposed to be getting from this. Thanks again for reading this. I hope you have a great day.

The next entry was a little more, shall we say, intense? Having issues with an ex-husband can be stressful enough, but when the issues affect your child? That is when it becomes ten times worse. Things were not always like this with my first husband, but I can't control the behaviors of others. As I have said before, our marriage was not a good one, but we managed to try to have a decent relationship after the divorce for Devin. However, we reached a point where things were not even at that point. I did not feel that he was stepping up enough as a father should, and I also felt that he was putting others in front of his *only* biological child. I knew that he was moving on with his life, and that those people would, and should, be important to him. I did not, however, think that they should be *more* important than Devin was, and evidently, that was where the issue was.

1/10/2011

"Monday Monday—so good to me—Monday Monday it was all I hoped it would be…"

Now who sings that song?

Anyway—Monday—another week—more —more irritations—and of course—we still have the whole week left to go!

Still have my headache—so far the meds have helped and it's not as bad as it was – but still lingering on.

And angry as can be at my ex—he spends no time with Devin—and he hasn't in two years—no cards on birthday, Christmas, Thanksgiving, no calls, nothing.

Everything started about four years ago when he started seeing the woman who is now his wife. It was just here and there that he wouldn't call when he said he would, or he would ask to reschedule a weekend for whatever reason, etc. Then he moved to the same town we live in—like five minutes —and things got worse— why you ask? Because she lives in the same town too! He was still taking Devin on his weekends—but rarely calling, and not having much contact at all during the week. Which this made no sense, since he only lived like five minutes away, and he couldn't manage to stop by and see Devin once in a while?

Then in 2008 around April—he says he's moving in with her—okay—no problem. What about Devin? She's got two kids and I was not about to let them just shove Devin into a corner kind of thing. I wanted him to know he was just as important as they were. I said he needed to have his own personal space—even if it was space he would share with something like the craft room, office, something. He needed to be able to have his own little area that he could go to be away from others if he wanted to. Just sleeping on the couch was not going to cut it. And until that happened, I told him he couldn't keep Devin overnight—but could still come get him, just bring him back before bed. This was not an unreasonable request, and they agreed. No problems, right? Wrong.

It wasn't until November of 2008 that it finally was done—and only after we had a blow up about it. He was bitching that he was not seeing Devin enough—

which was because he wasn't coming to pick Devin up all the time because if he could not have him over night, what was the point he said. So I gave him one week to create a personal and private space for Devin, or that he could take me to court. You had seven months—more than enough time to get this done, and once again—if you don't like it—then take me to court. He agreed, and finally the end of the following week, it was done.

He actually did it, gave Devin space, etc. I'm not sure what or why it took seven months, but Devin started staying overnight on his weekends again. Things went okay for a while, and then he went back to his old ways. Not calling Devin when he said he would, not stopping over, being late for his weekends, and re-scheduling his weekends, on and on. Now he always had reasons—but they were shit reasons. He couldn't call because he was busy watching her kids—which I might add that one is a little older than Devin, the other a little younger— but he had to watch them so much that he could not even pick up the phone. He would say that he was late because he slept late, apparently he did not know how to set an alarm. He would have to reschedule because he said he had to work—but yet tons of people would say that they saw him out and about doing things.

Then there was father's day of 2009. The last straw. He was supposed to take Devin for a father-son day—

just the two of them. That is what he promised Devin. They ended up taking his mom to church that morning—and who went with? Of course, her and her kids. Then afterwards they were supposed to go swimming and hang out—just he and Devin—and of course—those plans were changed—SHE decided that they were going to do things as a family. Forget the fact that Devin had not had ANY one on one on one time with him in about two years, who cares? Her kids are apparently more important. She even told Devin's grandma that he "has a family now" when asked about spending time with Devin.

Needless to say—the shit hit the fan, and Devin calls me from his grandma's house, crying, and I go over to figure out what's going on. They felt that he needed to just "deal with it" regardless of what his father promised, or what he said. When we left, I told him he wasn't going to be having Devin for a long time until Devin felt comfortable, and until he changed his actions, and those of his fiancé.

Needless to say—in a one year time, from Father's Day 2009 to Father's Day 2010—Devin only saw his father in person ONE TIME, and he talked to him on the phone three times. Nothing for Christmas, not even a call or a card. He called on Devin's birthday, at 2:30 p.m., when he's got to start work at 3:00 p.m., and said "I just remembered what day it is, is Devin there?" Fortunately, Devin was with my in-laws, and I told him, nope, and he just said, "Well, let him know I called."

Now come on—that's the best you've got? You couldn't even get him a card? And he did not understand why we were upset about all this! So I called him a few weeks later, and told him we needed to talk—face to face. Mind you, this is after we lost Mr. Man, so I am not really the person to mess with when dealing with one of my children. He agreed to come over and we talked about what had been going on. The fact that he chose to ignore his child over and over again, has treated him like shit, etc. His only explanation? Everything would have been fine had they not had to take his mom to church on father's day. Everything was her fault.

Now that I have rambled on and on—I don't really feel all that much better, but at least the pounding in my head has eased up a bit, which I attribute mostly to the meds. Now I must try to get on with the day—school work to do, errands to run, phone calls to make. No rest for the wicked and I must have been really bad in a past life.

Thanks for spending your time reading my ranting and raving.

Now, I know that this one has more to do with my oldest than it does Mr. Man, but this post made me realize a few things. I realized that I still had other things to deal with outside of my grief and outside of my pain. That I still needed to handle other things with my other two children. When I wrote this, I knew that the time for letting my grief rule over me needed to end. It was okay for me to grieve, but I had just as much, if not more, to live for. I read some of these posts and realized that in all honesty, my life complaints weren't that different than others out there living in mixed families or even single parents. I just felt bored down upon by the world because of dealing with grief on top of it. Looking at that post, I realized that I was going in so many directions all at once, and I needed to try to find a way to focus on one thing at a time and get myself back on the right track.

1/11/2011

Okay—headache is still hanging on—I am ready to cut off my head—everything I eat makes me feel ill, oh the joys of a migraine.

Today marks eight months since Zack has been gone—which means there's only four more months until we reach the year—of which I have mixed emotions about. Sad of course because that means time-wise—I am that much farther away from the last time I held him, but also relief at the fact that I've made it this far, and that I know he would be proud of me.

Still—every day is hard—my dreams lately have become weird—no clue why—it's not like I'm eating spicy foods before going to bed, I am not watching scary movies, etc. They are just way out there.

In some of them, I am me, in weird situations that do not make any sense, and in others I am someone else—I look like me—but not my name—not my family—and not anyone or anything I know—so very weird. It's almost like watching a bio movie of someone else, and you can relate to some of the things going on— but not all of it makes sense.

It almost feels like I am missing something and my dreams are trying to tell me what it is, I'm just not sure why.

Here's to hoping my migraine goes away, and my day goes better today than yesterday.

I never did sort through the dreams. I have never had dreams like that where they never eventually make sense. I believed that I needed to change up some things in my life, which I started doing just that shortly after I wrote that post.

The following day was a letter to Zack. I stopped questioning a long time ago why I had the urge to write the things I did, so I would just go with the flow when things like this happened. It was much easier to just get the words out than to be muddled and not have an outlet.

1/13/2011

Dearest Zackary,

Oh, Mr. Man, I miss you so much. Today, yesterday, and every day since that last day you spent with us. My heart just hurts so much, and I just love you so damn much it's just not right. I want to hold you, I want to kiss you, I want to hug you, sing to you, introduce you to new things, watch you play with your brother and sister, and I can't.

I won't say that it's not fair because I learned a long time ago that nothing in life is fair, but dammit, what about things being right?

I still remember that last morning with you like it was yesterday. Singing to you, playing with you, talking to you, and dancing with you. I can still feel you hugging Mommy, I can still hear your giggle and saying, "Mamamamama," I can still smell you as if you were still here—and I know it's just my heart and my mind, but I know it's there.

And it just seems like since that day, nothing has gone right. When you were here and we were all together, things might not have been perfect, but we were together, we were a family. Now, we are broken, our hearts, our minds, our souls, and our home. And nothing seems to be getting any better for us; it just seems to be getting worse. I know it's not your fault. I just don't know how to fix it. Like the saying goes, we might not have it all together, but together we have it all. Well, we are not together, and I don't know how to adjust that and fix this enough for those of us still here.

Can you give me a sign to let me know what I am supposed to do? Just tell me the next step to get us back on the right track. You and your brother and sister are my reasons for everything, and I am stuck in a spot that I don't know what to do, I do not know how to feel, I don't know what to think, I don't know what to say, and I sure as hell do not know how to act.

I know that one day I will see you and hold you again. Until that day, I will be broken and lost and have a hole in my heart, but until then, I need you to help Mommy get through every day and every step. Help me learn to heal. Help me take the steps that are going to put us back to where we need to be.

A piece of you is always with me and always will be. The problem is, a piece of me went with you on that day after you left us and always will be with you.

I need you to always know that Mommy did everything she could to save you and keep you with me. That was not what was meant to be, and I am trying to accept that. I need to know that you understand that, and I need you to guide me until that day you guide me back to you. That is not going to be for a long time, so you have got your work cut out for you, but I know you can do it, you are my son, and I know our bond goes deeper than life or death can ever change or alter.

So, Mr. Man, guide me, help me, and when it's time, welcome me home. In the meantime, help me in taking care of things here.

I love you, always have, and always will.

Love,
Mommy

I knew what I needed to get done, but I did not know how to do it. I wanted so much to be able to say, "I can do this," but I needed the knowledge first. I was so emotionally and mentally drained that I did not know how to keep going, but I knew I had no other choice. I still felt a sense of peace knowing that he was not in pain, but I did not have complete peace because I was still *in* pieces.

The end of January brought us another tragedy to deal with: Devin's grandmother, my ex–mother-in-law, passed away. I know it sounds weird, but I had a great relationship with her, we were close; and even though her passing was expected, it was still hard to go through. It had not even been a year since we had lost Zack, and I thought it would be harder on Devin than me. I was wrong.

Leonor had been on life support the last twenty-four hours of her life, and when they took her off, the family was allowed to be in there until she passed. I made it about ten minutes before I had to leave. I had watched my mom up to the last few hours when she kicked us out of the room, I was there with Zack when I *knew* he took his last breath, and I just did not have it in me to watch another person I love take their last breath. Devin stayed in her room the entire time. I don't know if it was cleansing for him or strength or how he really did it. When all was said and done, my young son was definitely more of a young man.

I finally did another blog entry quite some time after she passed and realized that I was so attached to her. I still miss her every day.

2/13/2011

Wow—it has been a whole month since I wrote last, and what a month it has been.

A few days after my last post, my ex–mother-in-law went into the hospital. Now I am sure that many of you are saying "yeah, that's not your responsibility anymore" and you are right. But I adored her, loved her as another mother, and she was my son's abuela. I gave her so much love, time, help, and did what I could do to take care of her and give her time with Devin. We had a bit of a bond you could say. When she went in, she was diagnosed with pneumonia, something that many people suffer from every year, and recover from. However, with all of her medical problems, it was serious.

On Saturday, January 22, 2011, she was transferred from TCU to ICU, not a good sign. They said they were doing this in order to give her better treatment, because they could monitor her differently and closer once in the ICU. Okay, I think, good, let's get her some better treatment and get her ass back home.

They called back a little after noon and said that they had her on a respirator to "help her breathe better," and I said I was on my way. Devin and I packed up, grabbed my sister on the way, and we were up there in no time. When we got there, I found out just how serious it was. Leonor had stopped breathing, and even though she had a living will, power of attorney, etc. they still put her on the respirator because they only thing they saw was that she was a DNR—do not resuscitate. They did not notice the "NO LIFE SUPPORT" portion until they already had her on the respirator—which for those that are unsure of all this, that's life support.

And then wouldn't you know it—I was the only one there, with my son and my sister, and guess what—I was one of the people listed on the power of attorney. Great, now I have to make this decision, and my heart not only broke, but fell to the pit of my stomach. I then decided that since she was already on it, leave her on it for twenty-four hours. This way the family can be gathered and have their chance to say goodbye. Dammit, I knew when she listed me on that power of attorney that there was a chance it would fall on me to make a decision, but I was hoping it never came to that.

So then began the craziness that was then the next twenty-four hours. I called my husband to let him know what was going on, and to see if someone can come stay with Rachel. I called Ed and told him to haul ass to the hospital, and to start calling his family. Then I went back into the hospital, and sat with Devin and Kara— hoping and praying this was not the end.

Over the next twenty-four hours, I worked with all the nurses, and kept the family informed as to what was going on, did everything I could do to keep her family comfortable, eating, something to drink, etc.

And what is sad—I am not even "in" that family anymore, yet I wanted to make sure that everything went as smoothly as we could have it – because I knew the pain they were all going through. In fact, in most ways, I know it more and better than they do. What is even more sad—the people I felt SHOULD have been in charge—sat there like bumps on logs either out of choice because I had it all under control, or because they did not know better on what their role should have been.

In the end, they were not the ones that were important to me. Other family members were, and even though I was no longer married into their family, I was going to do what I had to do to make this as 'easy' as possible for them. And what was even more wonderful, was that those people that I considered important, returned that feeling, and told me just how much Leonor talked about me, and how they were thankful I was there for her before, and there for them now.

Talk about a way to really tug at your heartstrings—and there is no way they will ever know how much that meant to me, and how much Leonor meant to me. Needless to say, at the end, Leonor passed away at 11:55 a.m., Sunday, January 23, 2011 after she was removed from life support. She was surrounded by her family that loved her and that she loved, and most of all, the one person most important to her, Devin was there to send her home.

Talk about some hard shit, not to mention I was worried about Devin the whole time, and here my wimpy ass couldn't hack it. I had to leave the room and go back out to the waiting area because I watched my mother die, buried a son, and there was no way I could watch Leonor too. I know she understands, but it broke my heart that I could not be there for Devin. I am thankful that my husband was there with Devin until the very end.

The whole next week, we helped Ed with Leonor's trailer, and then the funeral was on Saturday, January 29, 2011, after which she was cremated.

Since then, we spent a week with friends because of that stupid winter storm, and all last week was spent playing catch up with school work, emails, house work, grocery shopping, etc.

Which brings us to this weekend…a very unusual weekend for us. My mother-in-law took both Rachel and Devin for Friday and Saturday night, and we had the whole house to ourselves. We spent the last two days shopping for the house, paying bills—and then spent some time with Kara, went to see Triv, and then finally home to veg.

Boy, nothing much exciting to report there. It was nice having the normalcy, and not fighting with kids— but not very exciting, lol.

Well I suppose that is all for now. Thank you all for being there—you know who you are.

Time started to fly by with helping Devin with school, job searching, interviews, family gatherings, getting together with friends, and everything in between. In May 2011, I finally caught a break and got a job at a local newspaper as a sales associate for advertising. This was what I needed. I finally was getting somewhere, and things were starting to look up. We acknowledged the one-year anniversary of losing Mr. Man quietly. It was a hard day to come to terms with. One year is not a very long time, but when you look at the realization that it had now been one year, 365 days, since I had last held my child, that *one year* seemed like an eternity.

It was hard to come to terms with that milestone of sorts. I had made it that far, I had survived, but I also realized that each year I survived would put me one more year farther away from Zack. That was a tough thought to deal with. I know that I am made of tough stuff and that no matter what I do, I can and will survive, but I still miss my son. I miss being able to hold him and hear his giggle. I miss being able to see all three of my children play with each other like siblings are supposed to do. I had a moment where I wondered how many of these "anniversaries" I was going to be able to handle before I went crazy. That was a tough thought to deal with.

At that moment, I decided that I was going to survive. No matter the cost, no matter what it meant, I was going to survive. I was going to show my other two children that we can do this, and that we can do this together. I wasn't going to let his memory be forgotten, and I was not going to let his memory be marred by Mommy losing her mind and going crazy. With that decided, I put myself into my work and into my family.

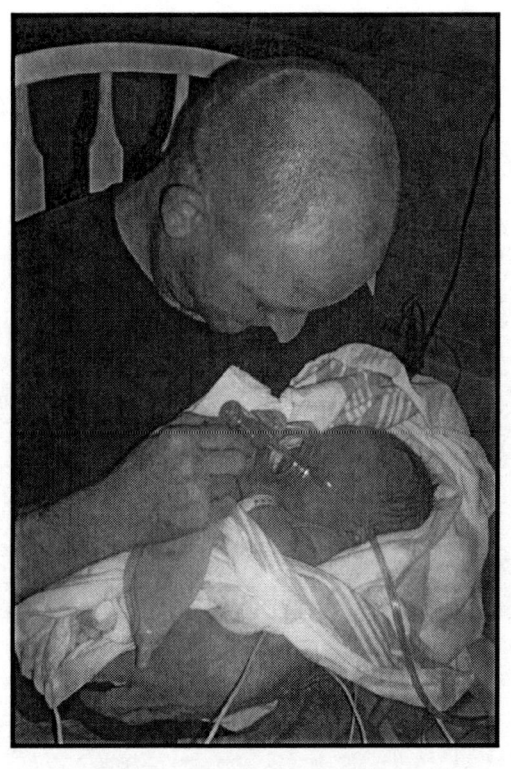

Uncle Mike and Zackary. He was definitely a proud uncle when he got to hold this little bundle for the first time!

Devin and Zack. There were moments
where these two were inseparable.

17

A New Leaf

As the year 2011 wore on, I started to find myself, a little piece at a time. I viewed this as a starting point to turn over a new leaf. We also started having issues with some friends and family because I was no longer the happy-go-lucky person I used to be. I was no longer able to climb any mountain without a problem. Every day was a struggle, every encounter was changed, and every thought revolved around all of my children.

At one point in the fall of 2011, a lot of things happened; arguments with friends and family and emotional turmoil made things very difficult. I took to writing again, and this is what I wrote on my notes:

I have looked back at my writing—and it's been almost a year since I last really wrote anything here, and can't even begin to tell you when I blogged last—so much for that New Year's resolution.

Been thinking a lot lately—A LOT—and for those that know me—you know that's dangerous. But thankfully—I have just been thinking about life—where I have —what I have been through—and what I have yet to experience.

And I think about everything I go through every day—the people I encounter—the issues I encounter—and I can't help some days that I just want to scream—scream at the universe—scream at people to shut up—scream at people to think twice before they speak.

I stick to myself most of the time—I go to work—I come home—I once in a while go to my sister's—and that's it—and why? Because I can't handle most people—I can't handle the fact that everyone around me tries not to mention our child we lost; because most everyone thinks I should just "deal with it" or that I should have "gotten over it" by now.

Well dammit—I haven't—I will NEVER "deal" with the fact of having to bury my five month old son—I will never "get over" the idea that I will never again hold him, hug him, kiss him, listen to him fight with his brother or sister, and the list goes on. The majority try not to mention him, think it will be easier on me, and it only makes it easier for them.

The truth is—it makes it harder for me—makes me feel like you just want to forget this piece of sunshine that will never shine on this earth again—makes me feel like you feel better forgetting that piece of my heart that is forever torn out.

For the most part—the last almost eighteen months—I can count to a low number, those that have stuck by us, and still support us, still talk about Mr. Man when I want to, let me cry when I feel I need to, and think about him openly every day. Those people know in one way shape or form, that my every day is a challenge to get up and get through my day without a tear. Those people know that losing Mr. Man changed me from a hard ass that could handle anything—to a person that cries at a stupid commercial.

Those people will read this and realize even more that every time I say everything is fine—that it is usually the farthest from it—but I know I have to keep on keeping on because of my other two children.

Then there are those that will read this and by the time they get to this sentence will be pissed off or upset—and to those people—I want you to think about what I wrote here—what might have pissed you off—and then think about why you're pissed.

And then think...

And think again...

And then FEEL why I am hurt—pissed—tired—angry—broken—shattered—changed...

An then take a moment out of your perfect life—and think about what you have done over the last almost eighteen months of hell I have lived through—and then think about where I have been—where my family has been.

And realize the huge chasm that is there—and when you figure out how to bridge it—I will be there standing at the edge—hoping and praying that the earth doesn't fall out from under me like it has before with my family behind me—all of us holding on together—because we are all that we have.

So we hold on together—and we hold on tight—and we stopped caring what other people thought—or said—because when it came down to it—we know we had to do this together.

And we know that everyone else was either going to be with us—or not at all—so I guess the question is this—

Are you hurting with us because you are with us?

Or are you pissed because you're part of the not at all?

And if you are part of the pissed crowd—once again—think about where you have been the last eighteen months—and think about where you have not been.

Love you, Mr. Man—I miss you every damn second of every minute of every day—You will always be a part of our family—even if we can't hug you and kiss you—you will always be here—and that will never change.

I did not call anyone out because that was not what I wanted to do. I knew that those individuals that were *not* part of the solution would take offense at what I wrote. I knew that those people would get upset. I also knew that there was nothing they could really say to what I wrote. There were definitely a few arguments that stemmed from this, but eventually, things evened out. I knew that sometimes you have to rock the boat in order to get forward progress. It sounds like I instigated arguments, but some things had to be brought out and said.

I had finally gotten to the point that I needed others to know that I was not going to lie down and play dead. I was not going to just follow the leader and let others dictate how I grieved, mourned, or even remembered my son's death. There are still, to this day, some relationships that are nowhere near what they used to be, but that happens when there is a death in the family. I knew that would happen, but it does not make it any easier to deal with.

My husband started working again in the fall, and as the holidays approached again, I took a new stance on things. I took every day one step at a time. Problems had begun to be a prominent issue in my marriage, but I did what I had to in order to keep the peace as best as I could. I planned only what I could control. We planned family time as we could around our work schedules. When other family and friends invited us to get-togethers, we attended them as we could. We never planned out very far just because we never knew what would happen.

The rest of the year passed without much fanfare, and 2012 entered on a fairly quiet note.

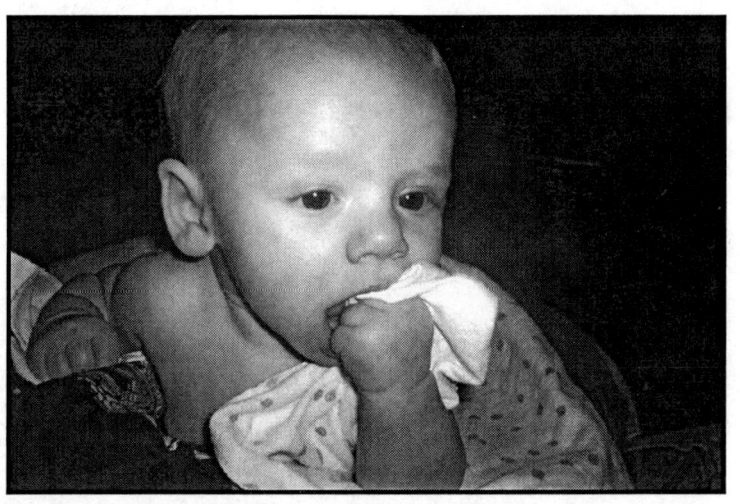

Mr. Man loved his blankies.

Rachel and Zack. She's trying to decide if she
should give him back his pacifier or not.

18

CHANGES

At this point, there really is no need for me to continue to give a play-by-play of events because you finally reach a point that everything begins to run together. Your minutes run into hours, into days, into weeks and months. However, this point happens at different intervals for everyone. I am, and have been, at a point that I no longer burst into tears every time I see another little baby. I have in fact been very active in the lives of some new little ones that have come into our family, and I could not be happier that I get to share in these precious moments with the parents. I no longer freak out and avoid the baby and infant section of the store. I do however still have my moments on those special days of the year that I should be celebrating with all of my children, and there is the constant thought that one of them isn't there physically with me.

I finally crossed that line from feeling slightly lost to striving toward some sort of purpose. I never lost sight of my purpose or goal with my grief and how to heal; I just lost sight of the path to get there. I do not believe in coincidences, and I do honestly believe that everything happens for a reason. I do not always have to like those reasons and I do not always have to understand those reasons, but how I react to them is the key. How I react to all of this sorrow and loss will not only show what I'm made of, but it will also show my children a positive way of coping. I knew, and still know, that by trusting in what I am made of and not worrying about the things I can't change, life will lead me to where I need and want to be. That is always easier said than done, and there are times that I falter, but I keep trying, and I keep working my way through.

Through my time at the local newspaper, I met some amazing people. Some of them I am still in touch with even now that I no longer work there. That job was a stepping stone on a career aspect and also a personal level. I mean nothing negative by that, but merely the fact that because of that job, I learned things about myself and those around me and how to handle them all. I figured out where I wanted to go for the next step in my life and what I wanted to do next. No one should ever view a stepping stone as a bad thing because it gets you to the next phase in your life and one inch closer to where you want to be or need to be. That is never a bad thing.

Early in 2012, we as a family experience another great loss. My husband's uncle passed away. It was a huge shock to the entire family. He had a history of heart problems, but things just went from zero to takeoff in such a short amount of time that no one had the time to prepare. His uncle was an amazing man to anyone and everyone. He was the type that would give you the shirt off his back just because you asked. His passing left another hole in the hearts of all of us, but the bittersweet moment was that I knew that he was reunited with Zack before any of the rest of us. At the same time, that knowledge gives me comfort that they are together.

After the loss of such a wonderful man, my in-laws decided for the first time since before my marriage into the family to get the whole family together for Easter. We need a reason to celebrate together after everything that had happened for the last few years. It was great having the family time together with my in-laws, even though my marriage had begun to fall apart on the fast track. It was nice to see the kids playing and having an egg hunt, and we even had a photographer come and take pictures of everyone together. That had not been done in years either, not the entire time I had been in the family. They are great memories that will never overwrite the sadness we have been dealt, but they will stand out and make us smile instead of giving us tears.

Also during 2012, some amazing things came into play. I've mentioned how much reading I have done over the years, and that, to be perfectly honest, is one of my biggest passions. Books of any genre, books by any author, even manuals and pamphlets, I'm more than happy to read. I started following one of my favorite authors, started talking to a few others I immensely enjoy, and that was all I needed. I knew that the literary world was going to be part of my salvation of sorts. I started talking to as many as I could, joined beta read teams when I could, promoted authors and books when I could, and I loved every minute of it.

I worked extremely close with Don. I knew his sister-in-law from back before I even had Devin, and we hit it off. We started working together, and he brought me into his team to promote his first novel, and I was so ecstatic to be a part of this huge literary world out there that I could have almost jumped for joy. It was amazing to know that I was finally doing something I enjoyed. Don gave me so much encouragement to do what I enjoyed and really helped me carve out my "niche" in a way in this bit literary world that surrounds us.

I then started working with other authors, became close with some amazing individuals, and they all really helped push me to complete this book. They pushed me to tell the story of Zackary, of my pain, my heartbreak, and my ongoing journey. I will be eternally grateful to all of them.

During that time, I found what I think has been one of the bigger epiphanies of all since losing Mr. Man. That is the fact that I really am a survivor. I realized that there are those people in my life that will be with me for a short time on my path, others that started with me and left, and others that joined and seem to be in it for the long haul. Each person I have encountered in my life has taught me something. I know that sounds cliché, but it is true. Of those that have left, I have learned how I do not want to be or how I need to change. Of those that stayed, they have taught me amazing things about myself. They have helped me learn that I have changed, but that does not mean something negative, it means just that: change. Of those that have come in "late in the game," they have taught me that it is okay for me to just be me. I do not have to alter who I am for anyone; I only have to do it because I want to. This also caused even more realizations, and problems, in my marriage.

In dealing with the death of my son, I realized that I changed immensely. It was not because I "wanted" to, but the events that unfolded in my life changed me into this different person. I can't say that I was at that time a better or worse person than I was before, but I was definitely different. I still laughed and cried, shared time with my family and friends, and still tried to have a good time when I could. The ways that I was different is that I stopped taking things for granted. The people I surrounded myself with both geographically and not, I made sure that they knew how deeply I cared for them. I made a point to tell people that I loved them. I made a point to tell people how much I appreciated them. I also made a point to show it just as much as I said it. That is the bigger deal, the "proof is in the pudding" type of concept.

I also started finding myself again. For many years, I lost who I was. I simply went through the motions, getting through each day just "being." I lost my sense of self and was for so many years the "wife" or "mom." I wasn't Tina or Kristina. I learned that I needed to change that, that I needed to get back to being *me*. I needed to learn how to be an individual, that I was a person who was worthy. I didn't want to lose what I had, but I wanted to be me again.

However, in having those realizations, I had others as well. I realized that my husband and I were no longer in the same book; we weren't even in the same universe in regard to our grief. He internalized his, I didn't, and things went from bad to worse.

In my search for self, I began allowing myself to think ahead. I still wasn't sure that I "had a future," even though in reality I knew I did. I knew that I had a destiny of sorts, but just wasn't sure what it was or how I was going to reach it. I wanted to help others realize that even amid their own trials, tribulations, and turmoil, that they too had a future. Yet how was I supposed to help others when I didn't know how to do this myself?

After quite some time and quite a messy situation, my husband became my *ex*-husband. We became a statistic in regard to families who have suffered the death of a child. The details of it really are more personal than ever needs to be discussed outside of those involved. We are both rebuilding, moving on, and leading our own lives. There are some Angel Parents out there that were able to create a stronger relationship with their significant other after the loss of a child, and there are others who split within the first year. Your relationship is something that only the two of you can know, understand, help, or work on. It is a two-way street, a constant ebb and flow, yet outside forces affect it more than we ever want to admit to. This for me, however, was a positive as I learned even more about myself in the aftermath.

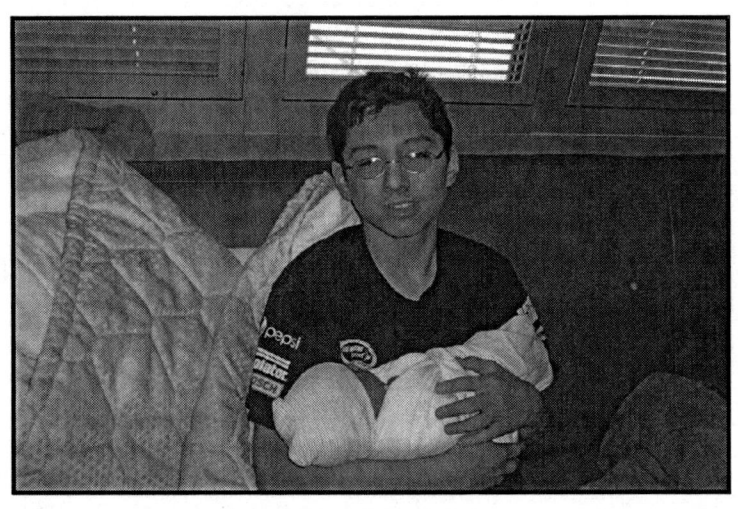

Devin holding Mr. Man at the hospital.

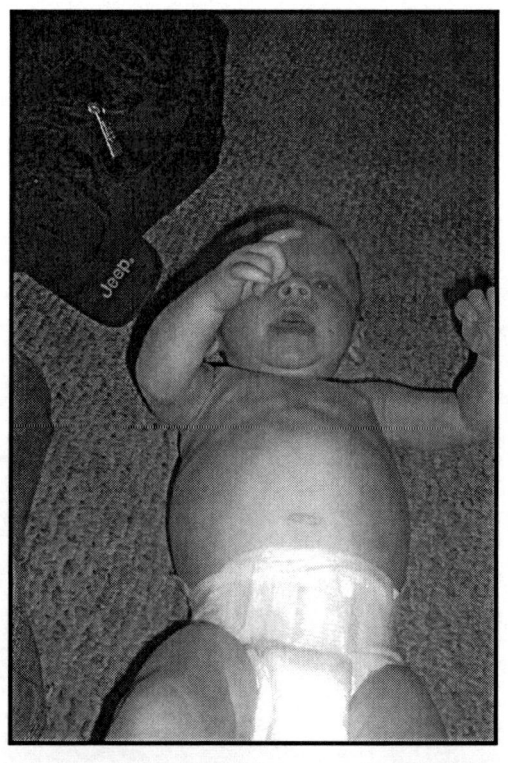

Mr. Man telling us a story. You may not understand it,
but he was definitely serious about it.

19

MY FAMILY NOW

Things all around have definitely changed in my family dynamic since Zack's passing. Some have been for the better, others I am slightly ambivalent about. I don't have the friendships I once did. That is both in number and people in general. I used to have such a large group of friends, and we would get together about once a month just to hang out, catch up, play cards, and let the kids all play. Now I have a handful. I can't say that I am surprised because I know that after a tragedy, it is difficult for some to deal with the aftermath. There are some people that I thought would stick by me no matter what, and they have not. I am not angry at them; it just makes me sad. I thought that the connection I had with those people was stronger, but life has a way of making you realize that you don't know much.

There are some that I have been able to make the relationship last; even after arguments and disagreements, we are still stuck together. One of the big changes was my marriage. We went in two completely different directions with our grief, with our coping, and with our interactions with others and each other. I began to find a new identity for myself. There are many Angel Parents who understand this loss, and many will go through what we did of each significant other going in a different direction. They are not alone in that, just as they are not alone in their grief. All relationships are a constant ebb and flow of *everything*, and sometimes you have to give 90 percent while the other person only gives ten and vice versa. However, in a situation such as this, where tragedy has torn your "norm" to shreds, things happen, and no one really knows what those things are or why.

My family dynamics became this: I have the ones that really matter close to my heart. Others I have known over the years and thought we were close are now more of acquaintances, and I have learned to be okay with it. I had to deal with the emotional aspect of why it happened, but when I looked at the big picture, I knew what mattered most and moved forward from there. I have forged new friendships that are amazing and closer to my heart than I can explain. Life is definitely about change, but how you handle that change is the hard part. The emotions that come with change are usually what everyone dislikes about it, not the actual change itself.

I had to learn how to be a different me. I had to realize that I am the only one I can change, and therefore, I am the only one that can make the decisions regarding what I do. I still worry about and care for my children, but the others in the world, they have to learn their own way down their own path. I can't guide them. I can walk next to them when our paths are close, but I can never walk the path of another. My children have their own path to walk as well. They walk next to me for a short time, and then they will have to follow their own paths.

As Devin approaches adulthood, I can only hope that I have given him the right tools to be able to forge his own way. Devin has been through so much in such a short period of time, and he is such a strong young man. He has made me proud, and I know he will continue to do so, even if there are days I do not agree with his decisions. Rachel is still young, and her path has already had its fair share of bumps, but I know that with guidance, she too will be able to forge her own niche and find her own path. She is such a bright and intelligent child that I know she will be able to find a way to let her personality shine. She has also made me proud, and I know that as she continues on her path, nothing will change that.

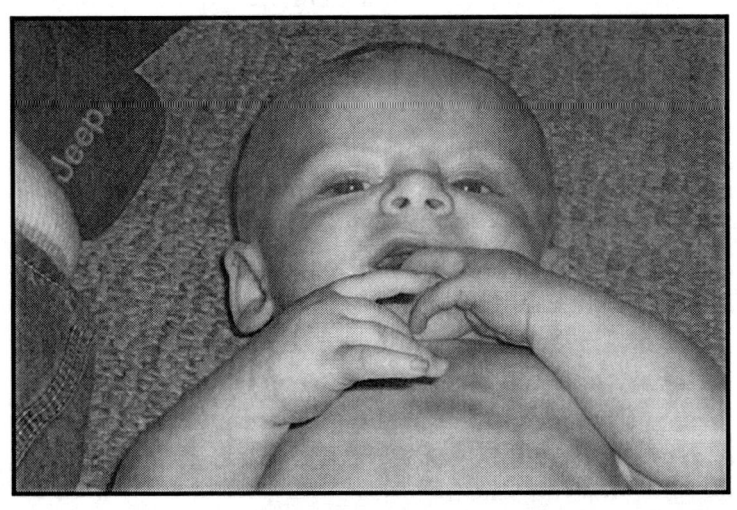

Mr. Man—always smiling.

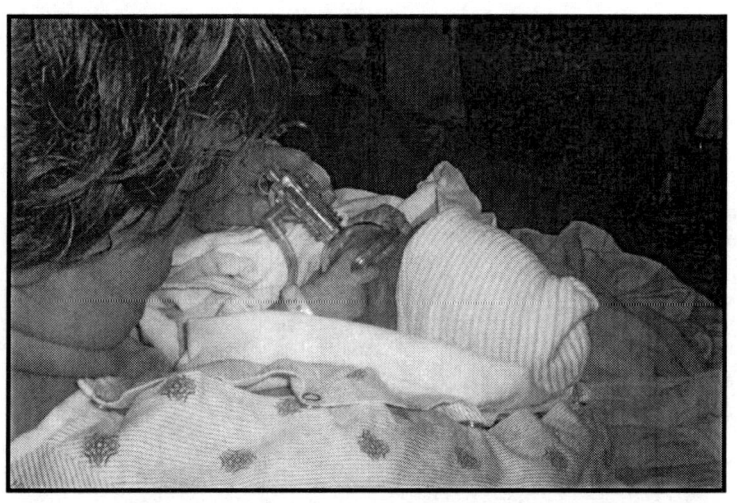

Mommy and Mr. Man during those first
moments after he was born.

20

COPING, CHANGE, MOVING FORWARD

Today, I am looking at a future that I never would have imagined. As I come to the end of this book journey, I see things unfolding before me. I have somehow managed to find a way to deal with my own pain by writing it down on these pages. Since the time of my divorce, I have a lot of changes that I have dealt with both personally and professionally. I had to find who I really was, who I wanted to be, and where I wanted to go.

I found my confidence again, not only in myself, but in who I wanted to be. I was able to focus again on what was important and who was important. Devin and Rachel keep me grounded to make all these changes happen.

Then at a point where I had decided that I was okay with where I was, who I had become, and finally wanted to work toward some sort of future, Chris came into my life and made me realize I wanted so much more. He encouraged me to follow my other passion and go back to school for certification in information technology. I never would have done it without his encouragement, and not only did I complete it, but I excelled. I have realized that it is okay to love again, even after tragedy. I have realized that it is okay to be happy again. Chris has helped me through these final stages of this book and has pushed me to keep going, even when it was hard to read the words I wrote.

While I may not have what I did, I like to believe that I have what is perfect for me. I am happier than I have ever been. Rachel and Devin are happier and smiling more than ever before. We as a family are more united than I thought possible after everything we've been through.

I'm not saying that all of this is because of Chris. What I am saying is that he was the catalyst that I was missing at that time. He came into our lives at a time that we thought we had reached the best we could do, and perhaps at that time, it was. However, with the addition of that one heart to this family, we have all excelled in our own ways and on our own paths. While Chris and I are no longer a couple, he is very much still one of my biggest cheerleaders and encourages me forward on what I want to do. We may not have worked as an "us," but he will always be one of my best friends.

I have dreams again like never before. I had reached a point where I thought this book was the last of my dreams, but with encouragement from Devin and Rachel, I have realized that I can dream again about what I want to do, what I want to be "when I grow up." I've started on a new career path I only used to wish for and, truthfully, never thought I would be good enough for. Now, I've not only excelled at the education and graduated, I have people interested in my talents and skills.

As a unique family, we have realized that there is nothing we can't conquer. We have realized that even though we came to this point in our lives because of our own personal tragedies and losses, we can still move forward. We have realized that we can still dream.

As I write this last chapter, I realized that for the first time since Mr. Man left us, I have hope—*real* hope. I still get emotional at times, I still miss him every second of every day, but it is different now. I realize that it is *okay*. It is okay to be emotional, it is okay to miss him, but at the same time, it is okay to be happy again, and it is okay to move forward toward a bright future.

This year marks six years that Mr. Man has been gone, and that means I have been working on the writings for this books for almost as long if you consider all my notes and blogs. Six very long years since I last held my youngest son. Six very long years since I last heard Zack's giggle. Six very long years since all three of my children hugged each other.

Our journey isn't over, not by a long shot, yet together, the family that we are now, we can conquer the world. I know that some will wonder what has become of the family and friends I've mentioned or my ex-husband, or wonder what happened to all the thoughts I wrote about at the beginning.

That is part of the change I've talked about this whole time. After the loss of a loved one, your life changes. After the loss of a child, the change is even more drastic. My ex-husband is dealing with his things his way, and I wish him the best. The family and friends that were there at the beginning, some I haven't spoken to in a few years, others I speak with daily. In both regard, they have things handled in a way that works for them, and I accept that. All the views I had in the beginning, of conquering the world, I still have them, just now the dynamics have changed of how I'm going to do it.

For those Angel Parent couples that make it work and you stay together, I hope that you always will find the ways to work together and make it work for you. You are blessed to have that person by your side from the beginning that you can have that total connection with. I hope that you never lose it, and that through the story of my journey, you can find something that will help you. You were lucky to have your family puzzle complete before tragedy struck. Know that even through your pain and grief and that part of your family is gone, and part of your heart is missing, your puzzle is still whole. You can rebuild your normal, you can redefine your future, and you can not only make your Angel proud of you, but you can be proud of yourselves for what you can, and have, overcome.

For those Angel Parents who have experienced not only the loss of a child, but then also the grief of a divorce, separation, or breakup, know that even though there are times that you feel totally alone, you're not. I know that at times through my journey when I felt alone, just me with Rachel and Devin, that it was hard, but those were times when I was able to find myself for what I wanted, needed, and could handle. Those were times that led me to be the person I needed to be, not only for myself, but for my children. That was part of my journey that led to me finding my path, and what I believe led Chris to my door. Know that you have the power to change your family puzzle at any time, and that you can define what it is you want, where you want to go. When the time is right, you will have someone join you on your journey. You were meant to walk this part by yourself, but you are not alone.

We are not as small of a "club" as we think we are, Angel Parents. We have been increasing in numbers every year since the beginning of time. There are Angel Parents that have been walking this path for decades, and then there are new Angel Parents that are just starting their journey every day.

We need to collectively come together and say that our babies are *not* forgotten, nor will they ever be. Collectively, we can change the views of the world on pregnancy and infant loss. This is such a taboo subject because there are so many people out there that never want to think about it. They never want to think that it could happen to them. I'm sure that each of us were at one point in those very shoes. It is now up to us to help all of those others understand that it can happen to anyone. Pregnancy and infant loss does not discriminate by color, creed, or age. It does not stay away just because you will it or wish it away. It can happen to anyone, anywhere, anytime.

It is up to us to help others, help the *world* understand that we are still human, we are still parents, and our child that we lost is still that, *our child*. The taboo will stay as long as we are silent about our pain and grief. The taboo will stay as long as we continue to allow people to tell us, "You were just pregnant, it wasn't a big deal," or "You can always have another child."

To Angel Parents, we weren't "just pregnant," and no child can be replaced. We need to speak up about our pain and grief, and we need to help others understand not only how to handle their own emotions from the outside, but also how to communicate and help us.

Our babies will not be forgotten for they live on in our hearts every day. Those around us know this, but at the same time, there is so much that is hard for them to understand. We have to help them because in the end, that helps *us*.

Together, we will be able to make sure that our children are never forgotten. Together, we will be able to help each other. Together, we can change the world, one heart at a time.

My past and my future—together in one startling image.

RESOURCES FOR ANGEL PARENTS AND FAMILY MEMBERS

These are pages and sites with information, jewelry, remembrance items, etc., for parents and family members who are grieving the loss of a pregnancy or infant. I hope you find solace or help in these pages, as I know I have. At the time I put these words to paper, these links are active, so I apologize if by the time you read this that any of these links no longer work. This is by no means a complete and total listing of all pages and sites available to you, so if you do not find something that works for you, please search, reach out to other Angel Parents, or e-mail me, and I will be glad to help you.

A Blog for Fathers When a Baby Dies
http://fathersgrievinginfantloss.blogspot.com/

Beadiful by Jennifer Sanchez
https://www.facebook.com/jenniescrafts

CarlyMarie
https://www.facebook.com/CarlyMarieProjectHeal

Christian's Beach
http://namesinthesand.blogspot.com/

Elm City Dad
https://elmcitydad.wordpress.com/

Faces of Loss, Faces of Hope
http://facesofloss.com/

Grieving Dads Project
http://grievingdads.com/

In Loving Memory of Babies Unknown
https://www.facebook.com/In-Loving-Memory-
    of-Babies-Unknown-179575808749966

Kayce Jones Designs
https://www.facebook.com/Kaycejonesdesigns

Miscarriage Blankets and More
https://www.facebook.com/MiscarriageBlankets

Mommies Precious Little Angel
https://www.facebook.com/
    MommiesPreciousLittleAngel

My Forever Child
http://www.myforeverchild.com/

Now I Lay Me Down To Sleep
https://www.nowilaymedowntosleep.org/

Project Sweet Peas
http://www.projectsweetpeas.com/

Skye's Bereavement Support & Keepsakes
https://www.facebook.com/Angelbaby.Skye/

Still Standing Magazine
http://stillstandingmag.com/

Honoring Our Angels
https://www.facebook.com/
    Honoring-Our-Angels-187843007934811/

Grieving Parents
https://www.facebook.com/GrievingParents/

Precious Angels Society
https://www.facebook.com/precious.angels.society/

Still Mothers
https://www.facebook.com/wearestillmothers/

Footprints On Our Hearts
https://www.facebook.com/
   FootprintsOnOurHearts/

Angel Babies
https://www.facebook.com/
   Angel-Babies-177888205646436/

Grieving Parents Support Network
https://www.facebook.com/GrievingParents.net/

A Bed For My Heart
https://www.facebook.com/A-Bed-For-My-
   Heart-144059799098261/

Held Your Whole Life
https://www.facebook.com/HeldYourWholeLife/

Pregnancy After Loss Support
https://www.facebook.com/
    pregnancyafterlosssupport/

Xavier's Ashes
https://www.facebook.com/xaviersashes/

ACKNOWLEDGMENTS

To my family, my friends, and everyone in between: thank you.

Without your support, I never would have finished this. There are specific people I need to thank because without these specific people, I wouldn't be where I am today without their support.

To Devin and Rachel—my beautiful children. Thank you for putting up with me while going through this roller coaster all over again to put it down in words. I'm not perfect, but know that I have always tried my best to give you the very best of me.

A special shout-out to Nathan, Megan, Crystal, and Joseph. That Saturday night that we sat around my sister's table and I had my breakdown, you showed me nothing but love and support. You made me feel that this was possible. This book is more than just my story, more than just sharing my journey with others, and more than reaching out to other Angel Parents who are dealing with their own grief.

This is about Mr. Man. His memory will forever be shared with others because of your final push of encouragement to get this going.

To Heather Bear—my partner in crime, chaos, fun, and love. I can't ever thank you enough for stepping out of your comfort zone and being by my side through some of the hardest moments you never would have imagined. I thank my lucky stars for you coming into my life and being my "little" sister. You are an amazing woman, and you make me proud to know you.

To my fellow Angel Parents—this is the most horrible journey anyone ever has to take. We are strong, we are capable, we are worthy, we are deserving, and we are phenomenal. Regardless of our myriad of different beliefs, we were given the opportunities to create these perfect miracles that were too perfect to stay in this imperfect world. We all will forever share a link with each other that only another Angel Parent can understand, and that is both a blessing and a curse. We are blessings to each other to have shoulders to lean on, and the curse is the hole that will forever be in our hearts.

To my niece Angel—a special Angel Parent. If I could change your path for you, I would have done so in a heartbeat. Nothing I can ever do will change the pain or change the past, but I will stand with you, beside you, and behind you. I will hold your hand when I can as we walk this twisted path. I love you, cupcake.

To Wendy—I don't even know where to start. For someone I have never met face-to-face (yet), you have been one of my biggest shoulders to lean on through this entire journey of pain and grief. You have also been one of the biggest cheerleaders in pushing me and encouraging me to do this. I am humbled by your faith in me, and I am honored and blessed to have you as a part of my life.

To Michelle—you and I clicked instantly, and it is definitely a connection that will last the ages. Thank you for being there to listen to me cry, bitch, and everything in between. I can't imagine that there will ever be a day without you in it.

To all the rest of my family and friends, I can't name all of you individually because that alone would take another book. Just know that each of you played a part in this, some with small parts, others with parts too large to explain. Regardless, each part has been important, vital, and more appreciated than words will ever express.

I love you all. I hope that whatever path you follow leads you to where you need to be, and know that each bump in the road is there to teach us something—whatever that may be. Know that sometimes you travel with a group, and other times you travel alone, but in the end we are all where we are supposed to be at the very time we are supposed to be there.

Lastly, to Chris.

You came in at the tail end of writing this book. You showed me that my world is full of color, full of life, and that I am worth every ounce of life. You showed me that even when someone is broken, there is someone out there that can come along and not only put the pieces back together, but also give them the glue—the *love*—to fill the cracks.

You have made me realize that I can shoot for the moon and that regardless of the outcome, I'm still worth it, still able to love, and I'm still landing on top.

While no longer together, I'm still thankful for you "jingling my line." You will always be one of my biggest supporters and will always be one of my closest friends and one of my loudest cheerleaders. I hope you find your happiness as I have found mine.

ONE FINAL LETTER

My Darling Mr. Man:

I write this letter to you, knowing that you'll never read it. Sounds crazy, doesn't it? Oh well, such is your mommy. I know that years have passed since I last held you and last heard your voice, but I still remember them as if they were yesterday. I wonder about so much. I wonder what you would have looked like on your first day of school, prom, graduation day, and the day you would have gotten married. I wonder how you would have tried to rebel against me in your teenage years and what crazy things you would have done with your friends.

All of those things will stay in the "I wonder" category for the rest of my life because you will never do them. It has taken me time to come to terms with that, but it gets easier each day. I miss you more than I can ever tell you, but you know because I know you miss me too. My life was never designed to be easy; I knew this from a very early age. However, I never would have imagined that it would have been this difficult to cope. Some days are easier—I can keep busy with everyday things, but other days…other days I just long to hold you in my arms, and I can't stop feeling that way.

You have such a beautiful soul, and I knew that from the day I found out I was pregnant with you. I knew from that first day that you were going to be someone special. Yes, I know that Devin and Rachel are just as special, but you were different from the get-go. From the day you were born, I saw something different in you, like you understood things we never would. Perhaps that is what this was all about. You came to give me a gift, an insight of sorts, and that was all. Perhaps you were here to teach us all something about ourselves, and your death was how that was done.

I know that each day that passes is a day farther away from the last time I held you, and one day closer to when I get to do it again. I watch Devin and Rachel as they get older, and I know that you would have fit in perfectly as you got older. You would have evened both of them out in your own way.

Devin still misses you and does things his own way. You would be proud of your big brother; he's definitely turned into a remarkable young man. He is far removed from the big boy he was when you left us. His age puts him at almost an adult, but from what he's been through, he's much older and wiser and, in some ways, jaded. There are things he has had to go through that I couldn't change or keep him from. He is still proud that he has a baby brother, but part of him is with you and always will be.

Rachel still talks about you when something comes up that sparks a memory for her. It really is remarkable as to how much she does remember. Unfortunately, the biggest memory for her is that you passed away. Hopefully as she gets older, she'll start to remember more of the stories that we share with her, and things will stick in her memory.

I wrote this book for you, Zack. I wrote this so that the memory of you can be shared with so many others. I also wrote this to honor the memories of all the other little angels that I know are with you. So many other parents have gone through the same pain I deal with every day, and I know that, unfortunately, more will come in the future. That is the part that really makes me sad, that other parents will know this pain of losing a child. I know that you aren't in pain, and I know that for whatever reason you couldn't stay with me, but that doesn't lessen the hurt or the hole in my heart.

Your big sister is in school, and your big brother is almost done, and I can't for the life of me figure out where the time has gone. The days go by so fast now, sometimes one running into the other before I realize it. My first thoughts of the day are still of you, Devin, and Rachel, and the same goes for the last thoughts before falling asleep. Since your passing, I have met some amazing people, and I tell them about you, the joy you brought to me, and the things I've had to learn since you've been gone. I think you have your own little fan club of sorts. So many of these amazing people have been part of the driving force of telling this story, and in some ways I think you brought them to me, knowing I would need them in my life.

So many of my dreams are starting to come true, and so many more are still in the making. No matter those dreams, nothing compares to you, Devin, and Rachel. You three are my absolute greatest dreams and accomplishments I'll ever have. I was given the chance to be a mommy to the three of you, and for that I thank my lucky stars. I'm sorry that you were not allowed to stay, the reasons I'll never know and probably will never understand. I do consider myself the luckiest woman alive to have been given the opportunity to have you as my son here in my arms for five months, and now, for forever in my heart.

Sometimes when I see other parents with their children and one of them is the age you would have been—it is hard. Not that I break down crying every time I see a child at the age you should be, but knowing that I should have you with me and that you would be that age, doing those things, that makes my heart ache. I want to go up to these young mothers who look frazzled from the antics of their toddler or young child and tell them to hug their children a little tighter, tell them that they love them, and get as many pictures as possible.

However, I'm sure that they would think I was an escapee from a mental ward and just ignore me. Other parents don't understand this pain unless they've been through it, and I really wish that there was a way to stop this pain from happening to others. I know I'm strong, but losing you broke something inside me. I'm not the person I was. Losing you changed me on such a deep and fundamental level that I'll never be that person again. On another level, losing you and the healing and coping since then has made me a different person that perhaps I should have been all along and didn't know it—at least not until recently.

Someday I will see you again. Someday we will be together and never again be apart. Until that day, listen to Grandma Kitti. I know that she is with you, loving you only the way a grandma could. I have to take care of Devin and Rachel, make sure that they learn how to be responsible adults, and make sure that they have as many memories of you as I can possibly give them. I still have a lifetime of memories to give them with other things. I need to make sure that their memories of their childhood, and their pending adulthood, will last long after I'm gone.

I'll admit, some days it is difficult to remember the sound of your giggle, and other days I can recall it without even trying. One day I won't have to worry about remembering it because I'll be with you, and I'll be able to hear it every day. That is a long ways away; I'm not old and gray yet, but until then…

Until then I will strive to be the best mom I can be to Rachel and Devin. I will work hard at making sure your memory lives on. I will put myself out there for other Angel Parents as the need arises because they need to know that they are not alone. I will show others that this is a tragedy, but that doesn't mean the grieving parents are less parents. I will do all of this to honor your memory and prove to Rachel and Devin that we are survivors.

I love you, my baby boy. I always have, and I always will. I loved you before I knew you were you, and I'll love you until my last breath and beyond. Meet me with open arms on that special day. It won't be for a long while, but I'll see you when I get there. Tell Grandma Kitti I'll catch her on the flip side, and she better be ready to dance.

With all my love, now and forever,
Mommy

CPSIA information can be obtained
at www.ICGtesting.com
Printed in the USA
FFOW05n2123050916